Straightening The Curve

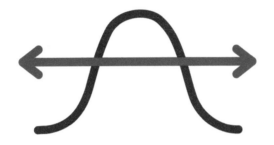

DESIGNING FOR DEEP LEARNING
AND CREATING THRIVING
LEARNING COMMUNITIES

WRITTEN BY
DR. KEITH KELLY PhD
DR. PATRICK WARD PhD

KELLY WARD PUBLISHING
Cleveland, Ohio

Kelly Ward Publishing
Cleveland, Ohio
kwk5882@gmail.com

First Printing: 2023
ISBN 978-1-387-50976-8

Cover Design: Katelyn Kelly and Ariel Morel

Dr. Kelly and Dr. Ward dedicate this book to our families and students everywhere.

To our families, we are eternally grateful for your love, support, guidance, patience and sharing of wisdom, as we strive to do our part to provide relevant and meaningful learning experiences to all students.

We are especially grateful to our respective parents, who have instilled the love of lifelong learning in us.

To students, we are especially thankful to you and for the privilege of being part of your lives. You inspire us as educators and enrich who we are as people.

Contents

Foreword

The COVID-19 pandemic impacted our lives in significant ways. In the early days, we literally focused on isolating ourselves to stay alive as we were bombarded with daily statistics delineating the worldwide devastation. The pandemic influenced our social and professional interactions, our finances, and our educational institutions. And worldwide, there was a realization that racial and ethnic minorities, the poor and disenfranchised had higher rates of infection, hospital stays and death caused by the COVID-19 virus than white, non-Hispanic people.

In education, we also isolated ourselves for safety and quickly examined how operating our institutions needed to change. Schools, colleges, and universities, whether public or private, had to focus on reimagining teaching and learning. Historically, the wheels of educational change move slowly as we discuss and eventually enact changes. With the pandemic, we were forced to examine our various circumstances and adapt. More than perhaps any time in our history, we were forced to shift our thinking to truly embrace transformational change. So, we found ourselves not only literally fighting for our lives, but at the same time we had to inspire and give meaning to educational purpose or risk losing our students. In order to persevere and promote success, educational institutions reached out to engage all stakeholders to improve systems in ways we'd never previously envisioned. And with the help of one-time state and federal COVID-19 relief funding, investments were made in technology, professional development, and additional support services.

Throughout Dr. Kelly and Dr. Ward's book, the authors help us as educators, experience ways of creating and engaging students in "deep and meaningful learning." The chapters explore change and growth that benefit students and empower teachers and administrators. The innovative methodologies collectively affirm the power of interventions built on a framework of strength and resiliency for students and the teachers. Moreover, the school board, integral to overall success, must support the changes and be actively engaged in understanding what works and what doesn't work and why.

A central element of the book centers around the importance of *access* to learning as a right and privilege for all. Moreover, the authors note that, "while a crisis will bring out the worst in us, it will also bring out the best in us—*if we allow it!*" More than espousing inspiring philosophical discourse and theoretical paradigms, real-life narratives recount actual examples of improvement and change. Contemporary learning must be designed to be engaging and relevant. Without relevancy, especially for students who are not usually motivated, our education system risks sinking into its own morass.

In education, we must never take our "eyes off the prize." That prize is the success of our students, teachers, staff, and administrators. We know that one courageous step begets another and one success generally begets another and another. Therefore, we must be highly motivated, courageous, and passionate. And, the transformational process must be holistic, embrace equity and interrogate the journey of all our students. As educators, we must take responsibility, learn from our failures, and embrace transformative change leading to renewed interconnectedness that helps everyone to realize their full potential. Much too often in education, we keep doing the same thing, expecting different results. This book challenges all of us to explore a different way of teaching and learning with an actionable vision.

Gloria J. Gibson, PhD
President, Northeastern Illinois University, Chicago

Acknowledgments

We would like to thank the many amazing students, community leaders, business leaders, parents, educators, board members and staff for their unwavering commitment, passion and dedication to educating children and young adults with great skill, care and compassion. We have had the honor and privilege of working with hundreds of exceptionally talented people of high character and intellect throughout our careers. It is these people who continue to shape our thinking and encourage our growth as we journey forward down the path of influencing others on how to design systems and work with stakeholders in order to engage students in deep, relevant, and meaningful learning.

In addition, we would especially like to thank the incredible school board, teachers, staff, administrators, students, and community of Mayfield City Schools. It is their expertise and love for students that continue to turn a vision into a plan and a plan into practice. Their willingness to research, reflect, design, try, assess and redo has resulted in the authentic and rigorous learning experiences we describe in this book, with much more to come. The leaders, students and staff of Mayfield have carved a trail of personalized and collective learning relevance that is fast becoming a model for others who dare to take the chance. With resolve and intention, the folks of Mayfield are moving far away from the industrial model of schooling. We admire them and are inspired by them. Keep Rolling!

Lastly, I would like to thank my friend and former college football teammate John St. Augustine for guiding me through this process. Your wisdom, experience, insights, and enthusiasm for our work kept the project on track. You have the heart of a lion and the spirit of a Golden Eagle!

We again say, thank you.

Keith and Patrick

Introduction

Dr. Ward and I wrote this book because we want to share our common passion, vision, and strategies for involving the talents of our school community in the quest for engaging students in deep and meaningful learning. We are extremely proud to share the work of our talented colleagues as well as the support we receive from an amazing community that understands what it takes to prepare students for success now and in the future.

It should be noted that when Dr. Ward and I began writing the book, I was serving as superintendent and experiencing all of the moments and work described in this volume. By the time it was finished, I had been retired for one year. The work of reimagining instruction continues to be driven by Dr. Ward under the leadership of superintendent Dr. Michael Barnes who, when assistant superintendent, was instrumental in laying the groundwork for improvement.

It was Dr. Barnes who once asked me the critical question, "*What is our instructional identity*?"

This book makes every attempt to answer that vital inquiry.

We believe that there is no better time than now, as we navigate the turbulent and confusing landscape of school reform, to move beyond the industrial model of teaching and learning. Professional educators have grown more comfortable in challenging conventional instructional practices for the purpose of innovating for relevancy. Information is ubiquitous, allowing for less memorization and more critical thinking. The science and research regarding how people learn and the connection to best pedagogical practices is robust and growing. Educational technologies are becoming increasingly effective and user friendly, making the customization of learning feasible. As educators, we are more willing to give parents and guardians access to the classroom and a role in the instructional process. Business and community leaders have recognized the value of our profession and want stronger partnerships with schools.

This book is about our moments and experiences as we work to straighten the curve for all students by reimagining school from the inside out. We have recognized the opportunities that exist believing and trusting in the research, the technology and most of all the talents of our staff and our diverse community.

We present our story as one that is ongoing and one that we are fully aware will never be finished. It's about lessons learned building the plane, flying it, and navigating it as it takes flight. In our journey we have found that panaceas and purported absolute solutions to the challenges do not exist and are nothing but a trap. A trap that will get an organization stuck in the very mindset from which we are trying to break. In other words, what we present in this book is not a complete and final answer, but in many ways, goes beyond the question of our instructional identity. It is our quest to create a learning culture that forever reinvents itself for the purposes of meeting the needs of its learners.

It is a place where all can flourish.

At the heart of our book, is the reimagining of instructional methods and engagement strategies. It is a way of learning we branded as All Access Learning. It is a way that is grounded in student agency, voice, choice, and outcomes. It is about equity, customization, and personalization. The All Access Learning heart beats strong and it is having a profound effect on our students, staff, and community. You'll be introduced to some of our core concepts. We call these concepts our *Distributive Leadership Structure* and *The Vision and Quality Improvement Plan*. These are models that engage the talents and power of our stakeholders and have proven to be an effective process for getting the work of innovation and improvement done.

Also, we present and discuss an outgrowth of our work we call the *Responsive Curriculum Framework*. A model that commits all of us to deep and authentic learning that is meaningful, relevant and rigorous for all learners. Laser focused professional development and growing our professional capacity is the glue that holds us together and is explained in direct correlation to our vision and our abilities to share and teach one another.

Finally, we share lessons learned and tales of success and struggle.

We invite you to join us on this incredible, ongoing journey in search of educational excellence. But more importantly, our hope is that it will make you reflect on your own journey and find our moments useful as you take on the work of helping students find purpose, passion, happiness and success. For these are the things we as parents and grandparents want for our children and what we as educators should want for all students. We sincerely hope you are inspired by reading this book, as we are by writing it.

Onward!

Dr. Keith Kelly, PhD

Dr. Patrick Ward, PhD

Chapter One

Building the Vision: Reimagining the Teaching and Learning Experience in Schools

Imagine a place sought out by children and adolescents because of their intrinsic yearning to discover and inquire. It is not in part virtual, although it could be. It cannot be found inside of a device, even though that could help. The place has no front or back and maybe no walls, no cognitive, emotional, and physical boundaries literally or figuratively. Its natural expectations are those of rigor, worth, ownership, hope and challenge. It has the feel of belief and the quest for finding real life passion reigns throughout. A place where every student is everyone's student, every day.

Technology and informational access, makes the present an incredible time to be an educator. Our understanding of how students learn is deeper than it ever has been thanks to the science of brain research and the trial and error of highly skilled practitioners. More time is dedicated to collaborating for the purpose of sharing and fine-tuning proven best practices. Technology allows us to customize lessons and units to the individual needs of the learners. Information is ubiquitous and learning can take place *anywhere at any time.* Artificial Intelligence will become a major game changer for those school districts that seek to refine classroom instruction utilizing thousands of learner data points.

An untapped resource for many school districts is the expertise that exists in the local communities. Small and large businesses, hospitals, governmental agencies, city halls and individual expertise, are amazing resources that can play more of a role than the occasional guest speaker. Classrooms become world class instructional settings when we learn how to open them to all that is available. Long gone are the days with the closed door and the papered window.

We know that most educators and non-educators alike have an opinion about what should be happening in schools. It can be frustrating listening to the shifting winds of what *should be taught* and *how it should be taught*. However, we need to listen carefully and identify the skills, attributes and habits of mind that will best prepare students for success through purposeful learning. Insights into realities from those working locally and around the world, can translate into authenticity in the classroom.

As educators, we spend a lot of time promoting the education our students receive, and for good reason. There are thousands of amazing public schools doing incredible things for their students, families, and communities. It is also true that public education is not only competing with itself as families shop and compare but is also competing in an education market that offers many alternatives. The importance of constant reflection on what we are not doing is as important as *promoting what we are doing*. This kind of reflection is not only important to meeting our competitive challenges but it is critical to our ability to adapt to the needs of learners and teachers.

All too often we get excited about a new educational initiative and because we have so much energy, time and money invested we may not have the courage to assess if it is working. Similarly, we don't often want to challenge the effectiveness or relevance of a legacy practice because of emotional and sentimental attachments. Vision, change, and improvement require challenging conventional wisdom in a way that uses multiple sources of relevant data to make the case for the why.

However, more importantly, it also requires inspiring a way of thinking that helps one to see new possibilities as a result of varying perspectives including those outside the schoolhouse walls.

Do Not Believe the Hype

As educators for more than forty years, we have sat in many classrooms and have worked with many extraordinary educators and community members for countless hours doing the work of strategic planning. The sweat, the frustrations, the joy, the debates, the hope, the dreams and the sense of making a difference, is an all-inclusive exhilarating and exciting experience.

Over the course of our careers, the hope and feel of the strategic planning document, three to five years in the making, in our hands gave us a sense of pride knowing that this time, something was sure to change. There was a deep sense that we've contributed to the advancement of our profession in a meaningful and profound way. It was a blueprint that was going to be the start of something that would change the course of a student's life and give more meaning to our professional purpose. The plan would be passed down and would surely inspire every teacher, administrator, and staff member. It would be their roadmap toward inspirational change and a newly found meaning to their careers. It would say to students we believe in your agency, opportunities, and access for all.

The plan would send the message to students, parents and community that learning is not a one-size-fits-all process but rather a customized and personalized experience. The plan would let students know that the classroom was going to look different because seats in rows are nothing more than an institutional pecking order. It would ensure that failure is not an option but a chance to prove yourself in another way. The plan would make it clear to all students that they are welcome and can achieve no matter their background and academic path up to that point.

But, during the planning stages there were no students at the table contributing to the planning process. Either a few adults decided for the many or a cast of many resulted in a watered-down plan. Agendas and politics blurred the vision. Practitioners were organized into historic silos, preventing collaboration and the opportunity for creative and innovative discourse. Courageous leadership gave way to "CYA" conversations.

Ultimately, expensive strategic plans sat on the shelf, while the power of the status quo sucked the life out of well-intended visions and goals for action. Leaders came and went. Communities divided. Budgets got tight. The hope was lost. In the long run, the absence of action resulted in a lost opportunity to reimagine how we do school. Discouraging as these experiences were, they sparked a different way of thinking about developing a vision and a way to make it a reality.

Moving from Ideals to Implementation

By design, our visioning and quality improvement planning process is anything but conventional. It is intimate, organic, and ongoing. Our process allows our staff to try, fail and redo at any time. We use consultants sparingly and do not engage large groups of stakeholders all at once. The process is action oriented and dependent on the expertise of talented staff to research, implement and assess new initiatives. We meet formally and informally with small stakeholder groups over the course of time asking questions and listening. Our process is not linear. John Paydo, an extraordinary teacher, and counselor described our process as one of a horizontal spiral with no end. As one of our then colleagues and courageous leader Joelle Magyar put it, *"We are not afraid to build the plane as we fly it!"*

There was no magic in getting started on an actionable vision of continuous improvement, just a little common sense and a refusal to go down the path most traveled. The first decision was not to call the process strategic planning. The term typically has a bad connotation among many and would create another "here we go again" feeling. The commonly used terms that many used when describing their hopes and dreams for educating children were: quality, vision, and improvement. So, we simply termed our plan the *Vision and Quality Improvement Plan* (VQIP). Our process for getting started was also not linear. Early in the development of the VQIP several action steps happened simultaneously.

We frequently asked stakeholders the essential questions listed at the end of the chapter. Stakeholders included students, parents, teachers, administrators, staff, board members, business leaders and community leaders. The settings were small, intimate, formal and informal. It is important to note that asking questions that require reflection about student success and instructional growth has become routine practice and part of the learning culture.

As we organized and considered the responses to the essential questions, the superintendent's cabinet team (district level administrators) identified issues and ideas that could be addressed immediately in order to gain some short-term wins. By doing so, we were demonstrating our commitment to using the thoughts of stakeholders to make change and improvement.

Essentially, the superintendent's cabinet team identified the low hanging fruit. There were obvious improvements that needed to be made to enhance student learning and improve our facilities. We did not need to wait until all of the quantitative and qualitative data were analyzed. A plan with a timeline and estimated costs was written in order to get to work. It was clear from our stakeholder conversations that much could be done immediately, without causing too much controversy. We wanted the staff and the community to know that we were action oriented.

Below are some examples of work that resulted in immediate "wins" and ultimately helped us to gain trust and confidence as we moved toward the more difficult challenges of reimagining how we engage students in learning:

- Installing a wireless infrastructure
- Installing air conditioning in all of our school buildings
- Installing a new student information system
- Improving the grounds around our buildings
- Adding advanced placement courses
- Enhancing our social media presence
- Safety and crisis training for all staff and students
- Enhanced security systems

While we simultaneously engaged stakeholders and set out to improve systems, our administrative and cabinet teams began reflecting on their own capacity to lead change. This was hard work and took many group and individual conversations. Developing courageous leadership in oneself or in others requires deep reflection, a fair measure of grit and a growth mindset.

Our cabinet team, through much discourse over time, agreed on the following ten deep convictions that would guide our work toward developing the Vision and Quality Improvement Plan (VQIP):

- The heart of the Vision and Quality Improvement Plan is to prepare students for success as they pursue their passions and purposes, now and in the future. Classroom instruction is the bullseye.
- It is vital to know the potential land mines of change and be strategic in disarming them.
- The VQIP must be grounded in the answers to the questions of Why, What, When and How.
- Knowledge of best practices, continuous research and creative ideas are of equal importance and inextricably linked.
- Engagement, planning and evaluation processes must be simple, intimate, agile and adaptable.
- Staff and students must play a key role in motivating and inspiring colleagues.
- Leadership must *walk the talk and talk the walk.* Administrative leadership must have the courage to challenge conventional thinking and model innovation.
- Stakeholder engagement strategies must take many forms and not be drawn out.
- Action research and early experimentation demonstrate a commitment to instructional innovation.
- The VQIP is organic and ever growing.

The Quality Improvement Pillars

What emerged from our stakeholder discussions were organizational themes that fit into four conceptual bins that we call the Quality Improvement Pillars. The pillars are dependent on one another and hold up the work of the vision. They are:

- Student Learning and Academic Achievement
- Fiscal Stewardship and Operations
- Growing Leadership, Talent, and Professional Capacity
- Community Relations and Family Partnerships

The goals and initiatives that are developed under each of Quality Improvement Pillars define our work throughout the school year. Each administrator and supervisor build his or her annual goals based on the quality improvement goals and initiatives. The school board evaluates the superintendent and the treasurer based on the achievement of the goals and initiatives identified under each pillar. We strive for complete alignment. The work of one is interdependent with the work of others. As a result, leadership silos are broken down causing a powerful synergy of collaborative leadership, ownership, and accountability to one another.

The naming of the Quality Improvement Pillars is the result of a conversation with Bill Wendling, over lunch in Nashville. Bill is a brilliant, deep thinker with public relations, education, and engineering backgrounds. Bill had been hired by our school board to attend the school board meetings, observe the superintendent's performance, listen to the community, and give feedback. His objective voice was invaluable to us and soon he shared in the excitement to transform our school district. Bill forced us to think deeply about the meaning of the words that named the pillars and what those words would mean to stakeholders.

All too often, leaders fall into the frenetic trap of *"change for change's sake"* without a deep conceptual understanding of the change itself and the effect on others. Ultimately, Bill deepened our resolve and empathic understanding by helping us to find the profound and heartfelt importance of what we were doing and why.

The Beliefs and the Whys

Reimagining how we wanted to engage students in authentic, rigorous, and relevant learning experiences, began with the intuitive notion that we have many talented and creative staff, students, parents and community members with a strong desire to prepare students for a dynamic and ever-changing world. We came at it with the premise that our stakeholders wanted out of the industrial age model of schooling and into the digital/information age of authenticity and relevance.

Our visioning and quality improvement process had resulted in a powerful set of beliefs, ideas and dreams generated by stakeholders, as we engaged in a process of reimagining the educational experience. So why reimagine? And, what are the questions we need to ask ourselves in order to create a different vision for educating our students?

The *whys* come from *four central beliefs* grounded in *student agency, engagement, outcomes, and opportunity*. These beliefs are at the epicenter of the Vision and Quality Improvement Plan. We expect that every initiative and idea must be grounded in, evolve from, and develop around the following beliefs:

- We believe that all students in every classroom should have access to deep authentic learning opportunities that allow them to use both content and foundational knowledge to find and solve problems, create, collaborate, think critically, and communicate.
- We believe that a new model for education places the learner at the center of the process.
- We believe in a customized educational experience focused on each student's academic, social, and emotional development.
- We believe that by providing our students with a rigorous and relevant curriculum centered around innovation and creativity, our students will graduate ready to compete in a global society.

The beliefs help us to answer our whys. But, fancy jargon-filled belief statements do not often cut it for some within our schools as well as for many on the outside looking in. Have you ever heard comments like, *"well when I went to school ... it was good enough for me ... and I turned out okay."* Responding to comments and questions such as these require more than writing or committing to a set of belief statements. It requires asking ourselves deep and meaningful questions of practice, purpose and passion.

If we are being honest with ourselves, a rote, one size fits all continuum of methods characterized by the routine of lecture, note-taking and testing does not cut it in today's world. We are not saying that lecture is not an effective method and it certainly has its place. However, much more than rote routines are needed to engage students in deep meaningful work that result in the skills and habits of mind students need to be successful.

We were recently hanging out in our community pool with other retired educators. When the topic of the *"good old days of teaching"* came up. We listened for a while, and then someone made the comment that sitting in classrooms as a student in the good old days basically sucked! Back in the day, many of us were bored sitting at a desk determined by the letter of your last name. After thinking about it for a moment, this group of highly respected educators broke out in quiet laughter and agreed! Those folks who say it was good enough for them would say they were bored in school most of the time. Some would even say that the joy of learning was worn out of them by fifth grade.

The truth is that children and adolescents have a natural yearning to discover and inquire. The industrial model of learning fit when the goal was to get a good job in the local community with good benefits. It is our experience that by the age of twelve, students want and need to find the intersecting slopes of learning and doing because they are searching for and sometimes driven to find the purpose in school.

In what profession can you close the door and work in isolation and survive? It only makes sense that the more we share with each other and work together the better we get at our craft. Most organizations depend on a culture of collaboration and teamwork to adjust and adapt. Yet, we as educators are notorious defenders of the status quo grounded in isolation. Change and adaptability is often viewed not as something invigorating but as just one more thing to do. Have you ever heard these comments following a meeting or a presentation? "This too shall pass." "That was just the flavor of the month" or "We tried that before and it didn't work." Of course, the all-time default line... *"That's not in the contract."*

We get it.

Not all change is good, especially when it is for change's sake and not grounded in pedagogical research and best practices. However, we must continue to challenge the status quo by asking well thought out questions that get to the heart of how we can advance our profession in a manner that meets the current needs of students and our society. If we do not, then we run the risk of perpetuating the current trend of one size fits all instructional practices and legislative mandates born from our inability to adapt to what is relevant and needed.

Like any outstanding school system, the voices, insights, and viewpoints from those outside the walls of our schools should and do have a strong influence on our vision for reimagining school. Each school community has its traditions, cultures and customs. These should be recognized, lived and celebrated as teaching and learning transforms. We have found that the process of growth can be grounded in recognizing and honoring traditions.

However, students leave us and head out into an ever-shrinking world making the traditions of the "it was good enough for me" mindset insufficient. Success in a global economy consisting of rich and diverse cultures is somewhat dependent on a set of skills and attributes not often found intentionally embedded in how students engage in their learning. We must, with clarity of purpose, design learning in a way that provides all students with culturally rich and authentic learning experiences.

Students must experience the value of empathy, differences, similarities, voice and choice in every classroom, every day while engaged in learning. Doing this will help to prepare students for a rapidly changing world that needs ethical and empathic problem solvers and inventors.

Reimagining how it is we want to organize our schools around learning has many complex layers. We argue that the discourse around school reform and transformation has traditionally begun with the wrong focus. The typical arguments for reform begin with external factors such as school funding, home life, school board elections, community support systems and legislation. All critically important issues with which we need to be engaged but not as a starting point for transformation.

Attempting change and transformation from the outside in, is akin to building a house starting with the roof. Another way of making this point, is to believe that just because a district has spent millions of dollars on one-to-one laptops and digital learning tools, instructional practices will improve. *Not so.* All growth begins from within the core of the individual and how one learns to grow within their cell of practice. Think about this analogy. As a nucleus grows and the cell develops it begins connecting with other cells to form vital organs. Without this inside-out miraculous phenomenon of life nothing materializes. The same holds true as it pertains to educational reform efforts.

We have been asked many times how it is we've been able to make so much positive change happen, in relatively short space of time. It begins with a simple philosophy that is contrary to conventions of transformation discourse. For us the nucleus is the classroom. At the core of the nucleus is each teacher and each student within the classroom. So, we see instructional growth and transformation as starting from the inside and working its way out. We have found that influencing changes in antiquated policies, programs and practices are more easily done when there is a well-researched and student-centered meaning to the purpose. In other words, we focus first on what we as a learning community want to experience in the classroom, then develop the cell around it.

There are dozens of fundamental challenges and questions when it comes to developing the cell of school reform. But a funny thing happened on the way to the lab. Two of the more intriguing issues of reform surfaced. The challenges of time and learning and the physical boundaries of learning. We did not anticipate these issues surfacing when they did, but the issues led to very deep thinking about our current instructional practices and the structures within the cell that were inhibiting growth. If the nucleus is too close to the cell wall or walled in—the nucleus cannot grow. Below are just some of the questions with which our stakeholders grappled:

- Does time drive the learning or does learning drive the time?
- If learning drives time how does instructional methodology need to change?
- What happens to content coverage? More? Less? Deeper?
- How is mastery and deep understanding demonstrated?
- Should a student who can demonstrate mastery in ninety days be allowed to move on before the end of the required time frame?
- Should a student who needs more time to demonstrate mastery be allowed to do so without receiving a final failing grade?
- Does every student need to dedicate the same number of hours each week to a variety of subjects?
- Should we trust a student to adjust time, more or less, depending on what is needed?
- Should every student be doing the same thing in any given class?
- Where does learning take place and who determines where?
- What should the physical classroom set up look like?
- What is the impact of ubiquitous information on industrial age models of schooling?
- What are the consequences for traditional public schools if these issues are not resolved?
- How are issues of equity affected by allowing time to determine learning?

Educators have wrestled with these questions for years and have attempted to put into place programs to remedy the problems with some admiral impact. However, the impact has been less effective because policies like block scheduling that work from the outside in were often put into place before the deeper questions were explored, answered and acted on. Our process has been to ask and discuss these types of questions at every level of our Distributive Leadership Structure and in every All-Access Learning planning session. Our expectation and commitment are to not leave these important conversations without a plan of action.

Chapter One Essential Questions:

- What do you think kids should be doing in school to best prepare them for success now and in the future?
- What specifically are we lacking to provide the most meaningful and rigorous learning experiences for students?
- How do we best connect community expertise to student learning in and out of the classroom?
- How do we know when something is working?

Spark Doing!

Below is a checklist summarizing the big ideas of this chapter into action steps that you may want to consider.

- Research best instructional practices and go see them in action.
- Begin educating the school board on best practices.
- Agree that classroom instruction is the bullseye and all paths of improvement lead there.
- Determine your Whys for change and improvement and develop a communication plan for sharing the Whys with stakeholders.
- Engage the superintendent's cabinet and administrative team in discussion about core beliefs about classroom instruction.
- Collaboratively develop a leadership set of beliefs for leading change and improvement.
- Ask stakeholders the essential questions listed at the beginning of this chapter.
- Categorize responses to the essential questions using the Quality Improvement Pillars.
- Identify the short-term wins and get to work on them immediately.

Chapter Two

The District Leadership:
Distribute Leadership First, Structure Matters

Imagine a place where human interaction and individual contemplation are not required but generated. Generated by the human instincts in all of us to connect, to solve, to create and to innovate. It is a place where the work of one is important to another. It is the kind of work that not only prepares one for individual achievement, but also for solving the local, regional, national and global challenges of the time.

As educators, many of us strive to build a culture of learning described in the paragraph above. However, we often fall short because the many speed bumps, barriers and time constraints that can suck dry the motivation and the energy needed to create and sustain change.

So why is change so hard? Everyone wants to improve right? So, what's the problem? In our early years as administrators, we were certain that all teachers had to do was listen to us, follow our lead and change would happen.

Nothing could be further from the truth.

In writing this chapter, the words of Dr. Judith Soltis, former English Department Chairwoman at Homewood Flossmoor High School comes to mind. Her message was, long ago, this: Teachers cannot get to work until they have a structure and the capacity to deliver the vision. Trust the talent, experience and expertise of the staff. Provide a roadmap, the resources and get out of the way. Put the challenge in their hands. Be available to talk, brainstorm and listen. Distribute the leadership.

Dr. Soltis reminds us of five practical lessons regarding change leadership, that after many lessons learned the hard way we apply today. These principles are key to turning a vision into reality.

- Identify, believe and trust in your talented staff.
- Put in place the structures and supports for the staff, students and community to dream, brainstorm, debate, create and innovate.
- Create a safe harbor for robust discourse and debate.
- Develop the capacity to engage in discourse that ultimately leads to action.
- Risk taking allows for failure and growth.

It's All Connected

The ways in which people learn, research, dream, discuss, create and ultimately act is interconnected. A vision is useless without a *Distributive Leadership Structure* (DLS) to engage the stakeholders. Conversely, a DLS is no good without a clear vision. More importantly, the DLS must be designed in such a way that it meets the requirements of the vision. The DLS must evolve and adapt as the vision takes on life and needs adjustment. The process of engaging a vision is not linear. One thing does not necessarily come before the other.

One of the most meaningful concepts of the DLS is the notion of the spiral. A spiral consists of connecting and contiguous circles. When applied to a way of thinking about leadership, the circles of the spiral represent the many situations and circumstances facing leaders. The nature of the spiral is flexibility and interconnectedness. Remember the Slinky© spring toy? It made its way toward the mark because of the energy generated by its interconnected and flexible form. In other words, the administrative team is crucial to the form and function of the DLS because of the necessity to interact intimately with all situations and circumstances which in turn, keeps the work moving toward its goal.

Empowering teachers and staff to act at any time is essential in developing a culture where risk-taking is not only supported but expected. By simply saying *yes* to an idea that is in line with the vision communicates to teachers and staff that we as leaders have their backs. What follows is a natural inclination to want to talk about the experience and plan next steps.

Our DLS process is action oriented and dependent on the passions of talented staff to research, implement and assess new initiatives. Consultants, site-visits, targeted conferences and workshops are sparingly and strategically used to build our capacity. It needs to be stressed that being dependent on consultants and conferences for developing capacity and sparking creativity will have an adverse effect because it unintentionally sends the message that staff lack talent. Our approach is to give our teams a challenge, and encourage them to ask for outside help if they need it. We have found that this approach helps to establish incredible trust leading to an unleashing of innovative thinking. As we've said before, *don't be afraid to fly the plane as it is being built.*

This trusting approach is both rewarding and edifying.

Our core beliefs as well as the core components of our Distributive Leadership Structure remain essentially constant. The overarching philosophy of how our teams work is grounded in the principles of the Professional Learning Community model designed by Rick DeFour. Our district leadership team and our instructional leadership teams (one per building) annually assess goals and membership. However, some committee components of the DLS are forever changing. This is a messy necessity for sure but for good reason. We deeply believe in the sharing of expertise as it erodes conventions of industrialized isolationism so deeply rooted in our profession. When a committee is finished with its work, it may continue with another related charge or be totally reconstituted to take on another challenge.

The Distributive Leadership Structure (DLS) at the District Level

The purpose of our Distributive Leadership Structure (DLS) is simple. It is to advance and support the vision and the initiatives of the quality improvement process.

The people who are members of our DLS, at all levels, work together to research, create, determine, vet, implement and assess quality improvement initiatives. We do not purport to have the perfect vision as to what schools ought to be and do. We don't have all of the answers to our questions, nor do we have all of the solutions. What we do have are people who are committed to knowing what we do well, doing it better and inventing for relevancy through research, honest discourse and good ole fashioned trial and error. As a result, we have seen terrific outcomes in the areas of student learning, innovative instruction, professional capacity, operations and facilities and community relations.

Each of the teams and committees listed below receives professional learning in order to enhance their capacity to lead change. While listed down in a hierarchical fashion, there is great mutual respect within and between each group. Each group informs the work of the other. This helps to avoid what we call the "silo effect." The "silo effect" is caused by a lack of understanding of the vision, the action plan and meaningful, selfless communications. Mitigating this effect is a willingness, on the part of all members, to share and help others to implement new practices.

The Board of Education

It is commonly understood that boards of education have five primary responsibilities: serve as elected liaisons to the community, determine policy, financial stewardship, hire/fire the superintendent and hire/fire the treasurer. We, however, see our school board as active participants in the Distributive Leadership Structure (DLS). As supporters of the vision and Quality Improvement Pillars, the school board provides encouragement and insight into the historical and political issues of leading change. A crucial component is a dedicated school board. They are the unheralded visionaries of transformation. Without their deep and protective commitment no vision can stand the scrutiny and become reality. Below are several ways we engage our school board as part of the DLS:

- Public board meetings. Each principal and his or her team makes a presentation highlighting an initiative that is directly aligned with the vision and the Quality Improvement Pillars. Presentation topics have included blended learning, personalized learning, using digital learning tools, developing literacy, social and emotional learning, building culture and community, data to inform instruction, self-paced learning, community partnerships, business partnerships, project-based learning and redesign of learning spaces. Students and teachers are always involved in the presentations, demonstrating authenticity of buy-in and commitment. Our board meetings are videoed and broadcasted. The benefits of this approach are many:

  - It is another means by which to educate the board about best practices.
  - Staff and students are able to express their appreciation for the dedication of resources and board support.
  - The school board can publicly display their leadership by making comments on what they see.
  - Staff and students are publicly acknowledged and commended by the school board—inspiring further action.
  - The presentations set a positive educational tone for the meeting.
  - The broadcasts are another means for the board to keep the community up to speed on what is happening in the district regarding our vision.

- Public work sessions. Work sessions are a common practice in most school districts. Consider scheduling between four and six sessions a school year. Work session agendas should be crafted to be in concert with the work of the vision initiatives. The agenda topics are aligned with the Quality Improvement Pillars. Typical topics include financial stewardship, teaching and learning innovations, legislative and policy issues, facility and safety innovations and upgrades, technology integration, community relations and marketing strategies. Depending on the topics, all or some of the cabinet teams are present and engaged in the discussion. Aligning the board work sessions to the district vision accomplishes the following:

- Sustains the team atmosphere between board members and district level administration.
- Keeps the board informed of progress toward major vision initiatives.
- Allows for in-depth conversation and insights regarding changes that may cause concern among staff and community.
- Allows for the cabinet team to pick the brains of a wise and veteran school board before initiating an idea.
- Allows for the clarification of staff and community rumors surrounding the work of the vision.

- Committee Work. Consider offering school board members the opportunity to participate in committee work that does not typically involve board of education members. Two such examples are the Superintendent's Council on Innovative Education and the Community Action Committee. The former is a group of civic leaders, business leaders, politicians, students, union leaders, physicians and administrators that provide insights into the work from their perspectives. The latter is a group of parents and community members that is connected to the Ohio Public School Advocacy Network. This is a grassroots group that respectfully interacts with state policy and law makers as it pertains to education.

- Conferences and workshops. Like many boards, our school
  board annually participates in state and national school
  board conferences. What makes this common practice
  an opportunity for distributive leadership is that we as an
  administrative team commit to joining them and turning
  that time into productive work with a little (or a lot) of
  fun sprinkled in. For example, at the state school board
  conference we schedule working lunches and dinners. Some
  of our most meaningful visioning sessions and discussions
  have come over a meal. Several years ago, we invited the
  board to attend the Model Schools Conference. This was
  at a time when we were building a vision for teaching and
  learning that was much different from how things had always
  been done. Needless to say, there were many questions as to
  the *whys.* The Model Schools Conference helped to answer
  the whys.

The Cabinet Team (CT)

Mitigating the "silo effect" is foundational to the success of change and improvement and begins with the cabinet team. The CT consists of the superintendent, treasurer, assistant superintendent, director of human resources, director of pupil services, director of curriculum and instruction, director of technology and director of community relations. By design, the central office cabinet team is not traditional. They discuss, problem solve, and make decisions on all of the typical issues. What makes this team different is the way it works and communicates. They resist the urge to operate in silos, and all have equal voice regardless of the level of expertise or knowledge.

To illustrate the above, here are some common examples from our shared experiences in meetings. The treasurer (CFO) weighs in on teaching and learning practices and what students ought to know and be able to do. The director of community relations offers her perspective as a parent. The director of curriculum and instruction offers a staffing plan that saves money. The director of human resources offers an opinion on a branding strategy. The assistant superintendent making budget suggestions to the treasurer. The director of technology tells a bunch of dreamers that the community will go nuts if we go too far. The director of pupil services giving insights into community politics. And most importantly, all of them are talking the superintendent out of making a bad decision.

You get the picture.

The idea here is establishing a team culture where any of us can go to another and get or give perspective regardless of title and position. This should be standard operating procedure. This does not mean that decision making is a free-for-all. The team understands each other's job responsibilities and decision-making authorities. This also does not mean that everything is peaches and cream all of the time. In fact, it is hard, complex work to maintain this kind of working culture when the natural instinct is for everyone to close their doors and just do their jobs. There are many tough conversations in building and maintaining this cultural shift.

Conducting cabinet meetings and interacting with each other on a day-to-day basis is necessary if *and only if* there is a commitment to putting egos aside and making the vision a reality. The cliche, "change is hard" is so true. But it's even harder if a team does not value diversity of thought, critical conversation, collaborative chaos, innovative insights and productive problem solving from those least expected. A lot has been said and written about effective leadership teams. In our view, the biggest indicator of a highly effective leadership team is when the mission becomes greater than ourselves and all perspectives are welcome.

The Administrative Team (AT)

Nothing is more problematic when there is a disconnect between the district office cabinet team, principals, operational leaders and staff leaders. A disconnect caused by lack of communication, empathy and a prevalence of top-down decision making can cause deep mistrust and inconsistent practices. Not valuing continuous input and perspective from those with boots on the ground will keep planning documents collecting dust on the shelf. The administrative team is critical to the execution of an actionable vision and holding the Distributive Leadership Structure (DLS) together.

Our AT consists of principals, assistant principals, district administrators and classified staff directors and supervisors. We've tinkered, over the years, with how to best engage and organize this group of nearly thirty administrators, so that the time together is productive and meaningful. While not perfect, we found that the following strategies work best:

- Remind stakeholders that classroom instruction is the nucleus of the organization.
- Start and end by sharing positives and commending great work.
- The focus of each meeting is to advance the vision.
- Report out on vision initiatives.
- Engage in discussion, sharing and brainstorming solutions to vision related challenges.
- Take time to educate the team on finances, recent legislation, board policy discussions and union matters.
- Use breakout techniques and small group techniques for more in-depth thinking.
- Use videos and stories to inspire.
- Allow students to be part of meetings when appropriate.

The District Leadership Team (DLT)

The district leadership team consists of central office administration, building principals and union leaders representing certified and classified staff. Like the administrative team, the district leadership team has gone through a sort of metamorphosis. Over the years it has grown but has often struggled to leave underlying union and administrative agendas at the door. To put it simply, we strive to put aside the politics and egos for the betterment of our students and staff and to advance our vision.

Throughout the growth cycle, much has been accomplished but maintaining solid foundations of trust can be tricky and are dependent on constant communication and many variables. The bottom line is that for this group to be successful both administrators and union officials must *first seek to understand then to be understood.* As administrators, we have learned this lesson the hard way many times.

What makes the DLT effective is agreement on the following purposes:

- To focus on the big picture priorities of making the vision a reality and how it is we are going to inspire our colleagues to get it done.
- To serve as the communication filter/forum to deepen understanding around our big initiatives and legislative mandates so as to be able to explain the *whys* to your stakeholders.
- To determine where in the system questions, concerns and issues should be addressed.

These foundational principles are restated at every meeting. They are in some respects preventative measures that counteract the natural tendency to go into the weeds and get bogged down in minutia.

We recognize that administrative leaders and union leaders need a place to hash out the details of contractual issues and have hard conversations. To that end, we have a subgroup of the DLT that meets in-between DLT meetings. This group consists of the superintendent, assistant superintendent, director of human resources, chief financial officer, three union presidents and top union officers. This is a time to air some dirty laundry among key leaders and maintain positive relationships. Also, the time together enhances our trust by working through the nitty-gritty leadership challenges of accomplishing our goals.

The commitment to establishing a Distributive Leadership Structure that involves the school board, central office administrators and union leaders is hard work and takes time. There will be resistance, tough questions and some may not buy in. To make it work, the superintendent with support from the school board must be willing to commit to its purpose. The idea and practice of shared leadership as a cultural foundation necessary for getting the work done must be non-negotiable. Understand that this may involve removing leaders who do not share in this belief.

Chapter Two Essential Questions:

- What does the term distributive leadership mean to you?
- What is the overarching philosophy for engaging the talents of stakeholders?
- Are leaders with positional power willing to let go and trust the talents of others?
- What is the leadership structure that will be most effective for engaging stakeholders and ensuring sustainability of change and improvement?
- What role does the school board play in setting and establishing a vision?
- Are school board members an active part of the visionary discourse?
- Are union leaders at the table as part of the visioning process?
- What is done to broaden the minds of stakeholders as they consider possibilities for improvement and change?
- Are all the voices at the table of equal importance despite varying levels of knowledge and expertise?

Spark Doing!

Below is a checklist summarizing the big ideas of this chapter into action steps that you may want to consider:

- Assess the current effectiveness and ways in which each of the leadership groups work.
- Assess the communication patterns within and between the leadership groups.
- Introduce the concept of a Distributive Leadership Structure to the board of education, the superintendent's cabinet team, the administrative team and the district leadership team.

- Discuss the reasons for thinking about leadership in this way with all teams.
- Form the leadership teams if they do not already exist.
- Provide professional learning on high functioning teams.
- Get a commitment from teams that all voices are of equal value.
- Determine the purposes, boundaries and scope of work for each team.
- Commit to instruction as being the focal point of all work agendas.
- Align the performance goals of the board, superintendent, cabinet team and administrative team.
- Align the work of the teams around specific initiatives that are in line with the vision.

Chapter Three

Distributive Leadership First, Structure Matters: The School Building Leadership

Imagine a place where autonomy and collaboration are not just clichés, but are necessary to upholding the brilliance of professional human practice—not replaceable by machine or model. A place without locked doors and papered windows. Its conventions are not shackled by accountabilities created by those with no sensibilities. A place where leadership is something to be shared and valued.

Throughout our careers, we have witnessed and experienced the large communication gaps between well-intended and talented leaders in the central office and the school buildings. In our view, it is difficult and sometimes impossible to make significant and sustainable change unless central office leadership and building leadership are on the same page. This is especially true regarding classroom instruction and program innovations. A Distributive Leadership Structure (DLS) with clear, built-in, two-way communication methods often results in innovative thinking and creative solutions to challenges.

A powerful example of this is when our team of high school teachers and principals got together to talk about our vision for solving the problems related to the limitations of the traditional high school schedule. A huge and pervasive topic no doubt.

In time, central office leaders including the superintendent were invited to listen to the brainstorm sessions. While listening, it occurred to us that the issue was not necessarily the mechanics of the schedule but the elusive problem of time and learning. A problem that has been pondered for many years and an issue that has been attempted, by many, to be solved by changing the mechanics of the traditional high school schedule. Subsequent conversations between the central office and building office leaders resulted in our team of highly skilled educators to examine the problem through a different lens. The lens of the learner. Here is what happened.

The high school team began discussing the ways in which students learn. They reviewed brain research and continued investigating the power of leveraging technology as an instructional tool. The team began discussing important student-centered topics such as ownership of learning, agency, voice, choice and opportunity. There was a deep reflection of their own practices and the team talked with students about how they viewed the issues.

It didn't take long for them to decide to act.

What would have taken years to do in most school cultures a program was designed, staffed and ready for implementation *in one year.* The team with administrative, parental, student and school board support designed a personalized self-paced learning option for high school students in grade twelve. The student response has been remarkable with forty percent of the senior class opting to take their core courses in this manner. Since then, students in grades nine, ten and eleven have the opportunity to experience learning in this way as well.

To give you an idea of the complexity of the challenge described above, the self-paced learning option is highly personalized while requiring intense collaboration with teachers, other students and community partners. Project and product-based learning is a foundational principle of engagement.

The students plan their own path toward mastery and their progress is monitored on a daily basis. Teacher feedback is constant and teachers must be prepared to teach specialized lessons to one student, a small group of students or a large group of students. The curriculums are often integrated and tightly connected to learning outcomes. Students and teachers work and learn in a space designed for this kind of teaching, learning and presentation of mastery. State of the art technology including handheld devices, virtual reality equipment, touch screens and fabrication lab equipment are the tools of engagement. And, my favorite part of this whole thing—failure is not an option. Grades of F and D do not exist. Only demonstrated mastery is an option—however long it takes! In other words, *learning drives the time.*

This was a non-negotiable demand of the amazing teachers and principals involved. Students love it for all of the right reasons.

Without a leadership structure that fills the gaps of communication and trust visions like this cannot become reality. Our core beliefs as well as the core components of our Distributive Leadership Structure remain essentially constant. The overarching philosophy of how our teams work is grounded in the principles of the Professional Learning Community model. Our district leadership team and our instructional leadership teams (one per building) annually assess goals and membership. However, the committee components of the DLS are forever changing.

This is a messy necessity for sure but for good reason. When a committee is done with its work it may continue with another related charge or be totally reconstituted to take on another challenge.

The Instructional Leadership Teams (ILTs)

The following is a discussion of how we engage talented staff and students in leadership and ownership regarding the design, implementation and assessment of innovations that have transformed our schools. But first, it must be pointed out that the importance of the building principal in this work cannot be overstated. Without a team of principals that share a common vision and have the courage and the people skills to inspire and take care of the needs of staff, parents and students, nothing gets done.

We are blessed to have such a team. A tireless and extraordinary group of leaders that have incredible dedication and passion for doing what it takes to prepare those they lead in order to prove all students with what they need.

Instructional Leadership Teams are in place at every one of our schools. The membership of each ILT includes administrative, certified and classified professionals. Our ILTs are perhaps the most important conduit within the horizontal spiral of the Distributive Leadership Structure (DLS). This conduit that connects the administration to the classroom holds the DLS together. The work of the ILT is to provide leadership, ideas, inspiration, input and feedback throughout the system.

The ILTs were once called building leadership teams. We changed the name to reflect our growth as a professional learning community. As our culture shifted to one of professional growth, risk-taking and innovation so did the need to refocus our building leadership teams to that of quality instruction.

As the name implies, the ILTs' focus is on quality instruction and how it is we are going to continue to grow, adapt and adjust our curriculum to meet the needs of students. ILT agenda items and discussions reflect the building instructional goals which are aligned to the Vision and Quality Improvement Pillars.

The memorialized purposes of the instructional leadership teams are:

- To engage in setting the instructional vision of the district.
- To support the academic vision.
- To monitor the overall implementation of key initiatives related to teaching and learning.

Teacher Based Teams (TBTs)

Teacher Based Teams are another critical link in the Distributive Leadership Structure. TBTs exist horizontally and vertically across all grade levels and buildings depending on the work. We insist that TBT members apply the principles of the Professional Learning Community model with fidelity when engaging with student data, researched practices and curriculum design. The collaboration, expertise and depth of thought among the teachers in these meetings is impressive.

As mentioned earlier, the fundamental belief of our Distributive Leadership Structure lies in the confidence of leadership to put a problem or challenge in front of our staff knowing that the end product will benefit student learning. It is the work of the TBTs that brings agreed upon innovative instructional practices directly to the students. Very powerful!

Like most, our TBTs are formally structured within and between grade levels and buildings. What may make our TBTs unique is that, given the need, a TBT may form at any time. Teachers are good with this because it addresses a pop-up need or provides a forum for developing a new idea.

A great example of this is our work to customize and personalize learning.

Our Personalized Action Research Team (PLART) set out to research the impact of personalized learning and define it for our teachers. Their research and definitions were shared with our entire staff along with a framework for professional development. Two teachers, however, from the same school building at the same grade level became intrigued and set off ahead of the rest.

They met and designed a team taught, self-paced and personalized model of instruction for their third-grade students. Their achievement results surpass those of the conventional third grade classrooms across the district. Currently, personalized learning is a kindergarten through grade 12 initiative and several other TBTs have been formed to discuss, design and implement. We believe that the flexibility and culture of our Distributive Leadership Structure encourages action.

Instructional Program Committees (IPCs)

Essential to advancing the vision is the work of our Instructional Program Committees. IPCs are formed to provide definition, research, implementation strategies, program evaluation strategies and professional development recommendations specific to the committee's work. The makeup of the IPCs is forever changing. This is another messy necessity for sure but for good reason. We deeply believe in the sharing of expertise as it erodes conventions of industrialized isolationism so deeply rooted in our profession. When a committee is done with its work it may continue with another related charge or be totally reconstituted to take on another challenge.

Below are some examples of current and past instructional program committees that have had a significant impact on moving from an industrial age model of learning to a collaborative and customized way of learning:

- *The Instructional Innovation Committee* developed our Portrait of a Graduate. The portrait reflects the competencies that all students will need to develop in order to navigate and be successful in our rich, complex, diverse and digital world. Their work has also included researching project based learning and blended Learning. This was a committee of fifty teachers who wanted to explore ways to increase student engagement and increase learning relevancy. It was this committee that inspired all of the committees listed below.
- *The Blended Learning Committee* has defined and built our blended learning model that utilizes the 1:1 technology available to every student. Members of this committee lead the action research teams that experiment with a variety of blended learning approaches in their classrooms then meet to discuss and refine. This committee is also responsible for assisting in the design and implementation of professional development regarding blended learning approaches.
- *The Personalized Learning Action Research Team* is an evolution of the Blended Learning Committee. Their work is laser focused and involves researching, designing, implementing and evaluating best practices associated with personalized and customized learning approaches.
- *The Literacy Task Force* designed a guide that brings consistency of best practice across all content areas in grades PK–12. This committee plays a key role in designing the professional development, implementation and assessment strategies for literacy instruction.
- *The High School Time and Learning Committee* examines the issues of time and learning. They continuously research and discuss the concepts of anywhere, anytime learning as well as alternative scheduling options that provide students with greater flexibility. Their primary purpose for examining

this issue is to mitigate the negative impact that time has on learning and becoming. As a result of their work, four hundred high school students take self-paced core and elective courses supported by teams of teachers.

- *The K–2 Learning App Committee* researches and experiments with the use of learning apps as they apply to literacy and math instruction.

- *The 7th Grade Problem Based Learning Team* of which every 7th grade teacher was a part, engaged in a book study using, *The Innovator's Mindset* by George Couros. A teacher member of the Instructional Innovation Committee was the facilitator. Currently, Project Based Learning training touches every grade level in our district.

- *The 21st Century Learning Space Task Force* researches and recommends modern day learning spaces that support personalized learning environments that utilize 1:1 technology, virtual technologies and support personalized learning, design thinking and project-based learning methods. Their work has resulted in the redesign of over two hundred thousand square feet of learning space that mimics modern work environments.

- *Makerspace Committees* are present in each of our elementary schools. Their work has resulted in the dedication of classroom and media center space for students to be able to tinker, create and innovate using common materials and state of the art technologies. What students do in these spaces is well planned, aligned with the curriculum and considered an important part of their learning day.

- *The Mobile Innovation Lab Committee* consisted of student design teams, interested teachers and business partners. Their work has resulted in the conversion of a school bus into a rolling classroom that travels around our community to schools, parks, pools, senior centers and event venues. Adults and students are able to board the bus and experience virtual reality, 3D printing, laser cutting, building, designing and making.

- *The Superintendent's Student Advisory Committee* is a working group of students that research and engages educators, parents, community members, legislators and school board members on what the roles of the teacher and student ought to be in today's middle school and high school classrooms.
- *The Superintendent's Advisory Council on Innovative Education* is a group made of business, civic, governmental, health industry, non-profit and higher education leaders that comes together for the purpose of informing school district leadership about what students need today to be successful after high school.

Students are at the table interacting with adults sharing a student's point of view in almost every committee described above. Our instructional program committees are as essential as any other team of leaders. Below is a powerful example of a committee of students from the superintendent's advisory council linking up with a committee of teachers that ultimately resulted in improvements in how we engage students in learning. This initial dynamic exchange became a formalized practice known as 50/50 conversations.

More and more students play a significant role in our Distributive Leadership Structure (DLS). Several years ago, when district and union leadership were discussing how we were going to develop the DLS and advance the instructional initiatives of the Vision and Quality Improvement Plan, we agreed to form the Instructional Innovation Committee (IIC) as part of the structure. By design the committee was limited to thirty-five professionally certified staff that included administrators and teachers.

The charge of the IIC, at that time, was to research innovative practices that resulted in high student engagement and make professional development and implementation recommendations. The interrelated related constructs on the table for research were blended learning, personalized learning and the use of 1:1 learning devices as an instructional tool. The team was also charged with answering the following four essential questions necessary to reimagine student engagement at every level:

- What is the role of the teacher in the modern classroom?
- What is the role of the student in the modern classroom?
- What should the classroom set up look like?
- What technologies should live in the classroom?

Simultaneously, the Superintendent's Advisory Council was discussing the same above questions. Their insights and suggestions were incredible. We spent three meetings discussing and recording their insights. About halfway through the third meeting two of the kids suggested that they put together a research presentation for teachers. So, four students formed a team and crafted a presentation that would be given to the Instructional Innovation Committee (IIC).

What happened next was powerful.

The IIC agreed to give the students twenty minutes to make their presentation. The students had done their research on the topics and could talk the talk. The student advisory council also interviewed their peers and presented their findings through the eyes of students. To begin the presentation, one of the students had taken two pictures using her I-phone while sitting in class. The first, was from the last seat in a conventional classroom set up in rows. The second, was from his desk as part of a circle of desks. The contrasting views from each desk resulted in a lasting imagery of student perception.

Then came the question to the staff.

The student asked, *"In which of these classrooms do you think students feel more valued and are more engaged?"* Then she said, *"We as students know you care about us, and we love our teachers, but sometimes just the way the classroom is set up speaks loudly to us."* Needless to say, the committee scrapped the agenda and talked with the students for two hours about what needs to be done to increase student engagement in learning. Students are now members of several action committees that continue to advance our vision for teaching and learning. Most impressively, our incredible staff wouldn't have it any other way.

We estimate that at any given time seventy to eighty percent of our professional staff is involved in collaborative work outside of the classroom or office in order to advance our Vision and Quality Improvement initiatives.

Our Distributive Leadership Structure, as mentioned, has evolved over time. It is not something that happens in a linear fashion overnight. This structure is effective in our school culture because people were hungry to invent for relevancy and the time was right. However, change is hard and there are many failures and many hard lessons learned along the way. We share our DLS with you not to suggest this is "THE" way to make dreams and visions a reality but to spark a desire to expand your belief and trust in the talented staff around you and give them the opportunity to reimagine.

Chapter Three Essential Questions:

- What is the overarching guiding philosophy for dialogue and sharing professional practice?
- Are building principals instructional leaders or managers?
- Who are the formal and informal teacher and staff leaders? What do they bring to the table? Do they believe in the philosophy of shared leadership?
- Is there an intentional method for gathering leaders and staff to discuss practices that will advance the vision?
- What is the two-way communication method between central office administrators and building leaders?
- Is time made available for utilizing the expertise and talents of staff to assist in design, planning, assessment and implementation of vision initiatives?
- Are students allowed to participate in professional committee work?
- Are business leaders, community leaders, higher education representatives and parents afforded the opportunity for input and feedback on visionary initiatives?
- Are committees genuinely tasked with using their talents to make recommendations regarding program design, professional development, implementation and evaluation of effectiveness?
- Are all administrators committed to the practices of collaboration, team problem-solving, change and improvement? If not, what then?

Spark Doing!

Below is a checklist summarizing the big ideas of this chapter into action steps that you may want to consider:

- There must be a clear and well-articulated vision for learning.
- Introduce the concept of a Distributive Leadership Structure to the board of education, the superintendent's cabinet team, the administrative team and the district leadership team. Discuss the reasons for thinking about leadership in this way.
- Develop the Whys for building a DLS. Share and explain to all.
- Educate and develop the capacity of the school board to understand and appropriately participate in a Distributive Leadership Structure. This keeps their eyes on the big picture.
- Engage your central office team in dialogue about creating a DLS. Assess their capacity, effectiveness, needs and willingness to give up a degree of control.
- Engage your building administrators and classified staff supervisors in dialogue about creating a DLS. Assess their effectiveness, capacity, needs and willingness to give up a degree of control.
- Engage and educate the treasurer (CFO) as much as possible. Know what you can afford to do and not afford to do before you get folks fired up about the possibilities. Get the treasurer excited. She or he holds the purse strings.
- Engage union leadership by educating them on the purpose of a DLS. Strategically ask for their involvement in key committee work and leadership teams.
- Assess the communication patterns within and between the leadership groups.
- Provide your leadership teams with professional learning on how to function at a high level.
- Be strategic and selective when forming the district, building and teacher leadership teams. It is critical that these teams

are driven by a strong desire to improve and innovate around instruction.

- Thoroughly understand the principles and tenets of the Professional Learning Community model.
- Get a commitment from teams that all voices are of equal value.
- Determine the boundaries and scope of work for each team.
- Commit to instruction as being the focal point of all work agendas
- Align the performance goals of the board, superintendent, cabinet team and administrative team
- Align the work of the teams around specific initiatives that are in line with the vision
- The superintendent and principals should form student advisory councils. Each meeting should focus on teaching and learning and how students experience it. It is also an opportunity to get student perspectives on new initiatives related to your vision.
- When forming an instructional program committee, be strategic and selective when choosing members. Choose your best thinkers. Select, first, those who have been waiting to innovate and do something different. Sprinkle in a few fence sitters and allow them to get excited over time. Always include students.
- Use action research teams to test ideas and new practices. Use them to report out to larger groups and recruit colleagues to take a risk.
- Assess the effectiveness of your DLS model four times a year. Follow through with needed changes and adjustments.
- Get moving. If you wait until the DLS is perfect—nothing will happen. The purpose of the DLS is to make your vision a reality!
- Believe in the talents of your staff!

Chapter Four

Design for All Students:
The Responsive Curriculum Framework

Imagine a place where learning by heart is replaced by the heart of learning. A place where the written and unwritten voices of question, experimentation, argumentation and curiosity can be seen and heard from not only the dominant but also by those who hide behind a veil of irrelevance in the back row. A place where the tools of personalization and imagination ensure that every child is involved in every lesson, every day.

If you have ever spent time running (or walking) outside for recreation, you know it's an exhilarating experience. Unlike being outside, running on a treadmill somehow seems far less satisfying. However, in Cleveland, the treadmill was a winter-time necessity. Curriculum work aimed at improving test scores is like running on a treadmill. We were doing a lot of work but not making big progress with student learning. We did it all. Many times. Pacing guides, curriculum maps, I-Can statements, common assessments.

Every week our teams would meet and invest a tremendous amount of time and energy in running the curriculum race. In the end, we were going nowhere. Maintaining the status quo at best. We had no real evidence that what we were doing was truly making an impact. This is not the hallmark of a learning organization. In order to transform teaching and learning in the classroom, the curriculum and how it is designed needs an overhaul. The old days of waiting 3–4 years to "rewrite" curriculum just will not cut it any longer. A new approach, a more responsive approach provides the hope to bring about more substantive change. What we need is a Responsive Curriculum Framework.

Responsive Curriculum Framework (RCF)

Nothing is truly static. The world around us is changing in so many ways. This very simple reality led us to an important conclusion regarding the work we are trying to accomplish in schools. We need a curriculum development process that is responsive to the changing world we live in and the very diverse student populations we teach. Through action research, many failed attempts and a lot of trial and error a simple concept was born, the Responsive Curriculum Framework.

The RCF is a natural outgrowth of what happens in high functioning learning organizations. When leadership is distributed through intentional structures every leadership process needs to be explored through the lens of collaboration and deep learning. Curriculum work is no different. Curriculum is the bridge between standards and instruction. This link cannot be overlooked. It is the gateway into the classroom. Curriculum that places instructional design at the center is the sweet spot.

Any opportunity to engage educators in this design work gets us closer to realizing the promise of a true learning organization. For a century, schools have been chasing outcomes at the sacrifice of deep learning strategies. What if there was a way to accomplish both? What if there was a way to not only improve student outcomes but give all students access to deep meaningful curriculum? While this sounds idealistic, *it is possible.* At the core of this work is the need for a responsive framework that allows a district to leverage curriculum teams willing to engage in this important work. Below are four key steps that set the course for implementation of an RCF:

- Step One, invest in authentic collaboration
- Step Two, establish an impact orientation
- Step Three, commit to deep learning by design
- Step Four, commit to a responsive framework

Step One: Invest in Authentic Collaboration

Starting on this design journey can be daunting. A responsive curriculum framework requires that key elements get built into the system. The first key to success is a robust culture of collaboration from the district to the classroom. This alignment is crucial to the ultimate success of launching a responsive culture. Putting in the time early to establish the right teams across the system aligned with a clear instructional vision will make all the difference. Start with the instructional vision and build teams around it. The more inclusive the teams, the more likely the impact. One key note here, impact leaders can visualize the collaborative network they want to build. Begin by asking a simple question, what teams can be developed to support the instructional vision? Below are action steps to be taken in order to invest in collaboration:

- Develop the instructional visioning team and include many stakeholders in this work
- Ask the key questions:
    - With regard to instructional practices, what are we most proud of?
    - If there were no barriers, what do we want our schools to be for our students? K–2 Primary Literacy Team?

The answers to these central questions can fuel the work forward. From these original teams many new sub-teams can be created. These teams should be aligned to the instructional vision and priorities for teaching and learning. While not exhaustive, below is a list of potential teams that can be formed to involve talented professionals in the work:

- 3–5 Task Force to Explore ELA Instruction
- K–2 Primary Math Team
- 3–5 Task Force to Reimagine Math Instruction
- 6–8 Middle School ELA and Social Studies Task Force
- 6–8 Middle School Math and Science Task Force
- 9–12 Humanities Task Force

- 9–12 Math and Science Innovation Team
- Reimagining the Essentials and Elective Study Team

This list at first glance may appear overwhelming. That is not the intention. A district can control the pace. For some, using all professional learning time to engage the entire teaching force in responsive curriculum work may be manageable. For others a 3–5-year plan to launch may make more sense. The important part is getting started. Once the timeline and vision are in place, begin the work by engaging each team with the same core questions the vision team wrestled with. Again, those questions are:

- With regard to instructional practices, what are we most proud of?
- If there were no barriers, what do we want our schools to be for our students?
- For this work, add:
- If our instructional vision was realized what would students and teachers be doing in this environment?

The first work session cannot be skipped. Giving all members of the team time to work through the vision exercise frames the work and establishes a clear purpose for the work. Skipping this step will ultimately lead to systemic failure to see widespread change. Don't skip step one. Build the collaborative structure, establish the direction, *sell the why*.

Without a collaborative culture, curriculum work moves from being responsive to being static. This is why developing high quality instructional teams is paramount to successfully impacting teaching and learning. A static curriculum reinforces the status quo and makes change difficult. Work on collaboration at every level and be intentional about this work. Thus, it should make sense why step one is to invest in a culture of collaboration. What this looks like in practice has been alluded to earlier in the chapters that discussed distributive leadership. An exploration of how collaboration and curriculum work go hand in hand can lay the foundation for this transformative work.

Collaboration is a fickle beast. It is often one of the most misunderstood concepts applied in education today. Working together, for the betterment of a school district, sounds easy. As it turns out, collaboration without explicit purpose and some direction, ends up being nothing more than planning time. After the team has been built and the why and a sense of urgency has been established it is time to dive into the actual design work. What might a curriculum responsive framework look like? What might a document that serves as a curriculum road map and as an instructional plan end up looking like? This is created in step two. Establishing the impact orientation and unleashing teacher design work.

Step Two: Establish an Impact Orientation and Do the Work!

The second key to success is the adoption of an "impact orientation." Responsive organizations keep impact out front, all the time. As we work towards reimagining how curriculum is developed, we have kept impact on student outcomes as the most important factor to determine if we have been successful. The key to impact is to shorten the work cycle and make the work the work!

There is a historical problem worth noting here.

When we engage a team in work that doesn't help with instructional design or create anything useful the result is often a document that doesn't impact instruction. The goal here is short cycles and impact. After the team has gone through the vision exercise, understanding the purpose, has some urgency around the why the next key question we ask in the process is this, what would your next unit of instruction look like if it realized the instructional vision?

How does the role of the teacher and the student change in the next unit? Ask the question, let the team begin to design. The key to impact is having teams create something that they will use in the next several weeks. The first prototype or model curriculum should be something that can be tested and used. Immediately. Not in a year, not in a semester. Build something that will be used soon. The question that might be asked now is this. Is the unit a curriculum? The short answer is no. The unit will be used to create the core elements of the curriculum. Design first. Memorialize second. Even more critical.

Let the teams create, teach, return and then discuss. Through those discussions (modifications of the prototype) the curriculum components emerged and should be memorialized. The process is not technical by any means. The process leverages the expertise of the teachers and the positive dialogue that can emerge when educators not only teach but then reflect on the instruction after it occurred. The focus is not on creating a document, the focus is on creating model instructional units that when used allow everyone to stay focused on outcomes.

The end result of repeating this work throughout a school year is a complete document that has key standards, objectives, learning outcomes, evaluation opportunities and most importantly a model unit of instruction aligned to the instructional vision. The instructional model is the bread and butter. When we create what we will actually use, the time invested in the work becomes more meaningful. It also gets us closer to the heart of impact. The classroom. Quality instruction. Build the team, establish the instructional vision and let the team lose on designing their next unit of instruction. Work in reverse from there.

The cycle:

- Design a unit aligned to the instructional vision
- Analyze the components of the unit
- Teach the unit
- Reflect with the team on the unit, conduct the audit
- Identify key components of the curriculum
- Memorialize the curriculum and model unit
- Begin working on next unit, complete cycle until course complete
- Cycle 2: Adjust and respond to the learners needs by tweaking unit
- Monitor for impact—be mindful of outcomes

Step three is an important reminder on a key component of any instructional vision. Deep learning.

Step Three: Commit to Deep Learning for All by Design

Without question, the world of education has changed dramatically, and continues to evolve. Given the advent of technology and the unlimited access to information the need to engage all students in deeper and more authentic learning is paramount. The key here is all students and by design. If deep learning is left as an afterthought to something that happens after learning is done, nothing meaningful will ever happen. In short, deeper learning opportunities need to be embedded in the learning environment all the time, every unit, every day. In short, deeper learning is the fuel that drives the classroom of today. What we need is to pay attention to it without getting lost in the technical jungle.

As a side note, let's address the elephant in the room.

Our profession has a jargon problem. The technical jungle of education can turn off even the most accomplished educator. The trap is to stay out of the technical jargon. Once we get lost in the words the meaning and more importantly impact begins to fade. Don't make deep learning experiences about jargon. Don't over complicate it. A commitment to deep learning for all is central to a curriculum development process that places students at the center. When we say "*deep learning for all*" what we are committing to is making deep learning the driver of how time in the classroom is spent. We are also committed to providing access for all students, every day.

Deep learning includes more writing, more reading, more autonomy, more authenticity and more mastery. Most importantly, deeper learning makes *LEARNING* the variable, not time. Call it whatever you want. Select a framework if it helps. Most importantly design for it, then audit for it. This bears repeating: *Design for it*. Then get a team of professionals together and conduct a scavenger hunt. Search for deep learning. If you can't find it, design and tweak. Even more exciting, if the first prototype doesn't meet the standard, design again and try it again. The more we embed the work in real time and tweak the work in real time the greater chance for impact.

A responsive curriculum framework should keep deep learning as the focus of how students spend their time in school. Building collaborative structures, focusing on impact and keeping deep learning as the nucleus are the preconditions for reimagining curriculum development. Once these are in place, it becomes time to engage the team! The process described here is not intended to be linear, but ultimately designed to provide all students access to a rigorous, guaranteed and comprehensive curriculum.

The Cycle (revisited):

- Design a unit aligned to the instructional vision.
- Analyze the components of the unit.
- Teach the unit.
- Reflect with the team on the unit, conduct the audit.
- Identify key components of the curriculum.
- Memorialize the curriculum and model unit.
- Begin working on the next unit, complete cycle until course complete.
- Cycle 2: Adjust and respond to the learners needs by tweaking the unit.
- Monitor for impact and be mindful of outcomes.
- Make the changes and look for deep learning.

Ask the following questions:

- Do the students get to read deeply?
- Are the students producing a writing product? Is the task authentic?
- Do the students have a voice?
- Are students given the chance to move at their own pace?
- Where is the evidence of deep learning?
- Where is the evidence of critical thinking?

As a final note, when conducting the audit with the team it is important to hold each other accountable. This requires one of the key dimensions of collaboration, comfortable taking risks and receiving feedback. The worst outcome is that we don't find deep learning. The response is simple. Redesign the unit. A possible blueprint for this audit and organization is provided later as an example. This work should be fun. This work should be engaging. This work is about impact! Let our teams go, give them the vision and watch what happens when professionals design instruction worthy of our students.

The final part, step four is the commitment to this cycle when it comes to curriculum work. Committing to a responsive framework is a mindset shift. It requires some key commitments from the beginning. There are no shortcuts. The work upfront to build the team ultimately yields the results of improved student outcomes and deeper engagement.

Step Four: Commit to a Responsive Framework

It is best to dive into the work with a story and an example. As a district, we were faced with having to engage in both science and social studies curriculum work. Prior to engaging in the work, a design team gathered together to reflect on how to best approach this work, accomplish our goal and reimagine how instruction is provided for our students. We knew that we did not want to end up with a curriculum document that would land on the shelf and not be used. We also knew that the district was working hard to personalize learning across the system. The core question became, what process could support our current work and help us create a curriculum for all students to access.

The traditional approach to curriculum work is rather static. We knew that while elements of the classic approach were good, we needed an approach that would enhance the classic model and align with the overall vision. So, we formed an instructional innovation team that would over time establish an instructional vision for teaching and learning and created a framework to capture our core beliefs regarding the purpose of instruction. Action research study teams were assembled and the work began. The work of our staff took place before, during and after the school year. The work never really stops. Constant reflection, analysis and evaluation is organic to the process.

Our goal was to develop a process that placed our vision for learning at the center of the process. After years of shuffling curriculum, developing pacing guides and vertically aligning curriculum the need to rethink how we approach this work became clear. The result was to completely disrupt the traditional curriculum development process. We gathered our K–12 social studies and science team together and were ready to try a new approach. Like any collaborative meeting we began with our three core norms below:

- Permission to be uncomfortable
- Don't take this work personally it's about our students
- Act for impact, spark doing.

After a brief introduction, we took a few minutes to orient the entire team to work. The difference for this meeting was we wanted our teacher teams working on their next unit of instruction. Instead of getting bogged down in working on an entire curriculum rewrite all year with the hope of implementation in year two, we chose to focus on what we were going to teach in the next unit. We gave our team permission to learn through implementation. This is a subtle yet significant shift.

We moved from a 3–5-year plan, to an interactive and ongoing approach. The risk and calculation were simple. If we adopt a design thinking mindset and create a prototype, teachers might be more willing to tweak the design and view it as less static and fixed. The goal was to move from planning to designing curriculum. Prototypes are intended to be improved. We wanted a curriculum development process that had a degree of responsiveness baked into the design. What we ended up with was simple in principle and target in execution.

Then, we created our curriculum sandbox in which our teachers could then design. The sandbox was our vision for personalized learning. We developed tools for the sandbox to help them start thinking differently about our design work. You cannot build a sandcastle without the right tools. We created our vision (the sandbox), developed tools (responsive curriculum template) and we let our teams lose. The result, a personalized unit to take back to the team to use, tinker with and improve.

This was the starting place for our second meeting. Each of our Curriculum Design Institutes (CDIs) started with professional learning and sharing for the first hour followed by design time and teamwork. In other words, first the whole group is learning then back to the sandbox to design! Below are our questions for the whole group reflection:

- What worked well? Why?
- What was the impact on outcomes? How do you know?
- What would you change for next time?
- What learning routines need to be developed for students to be successful accessing this content?
- Can you incorporate those changes into the design you will work on today?

Committing to this process and framework can be transformative. Full system change begins by shortening the cycle and impacting instruction. Simple process. Major results when executed to scale. Start small and test it out. Go large and see the possibility. Either way, the worst-case outcome, improved instruction and a more coherent relevant understanding of curriculum. The following examples showcase what our planning tool ended up looking like. An important side note, teachers had input early in design session one and helped develop this framework. As we rolled into a pandemic, this simple design framework paired with a workshop model ended up setting us up for success, during an incredibly difficult year.

The Responsive Curriculum Planning Tool

In our sandbox we had two main bins. These bins were the tools we used to help organize content in a way that promoted personalization and deep learning. In Figure 2 below you will see core elements of our planning tool. In Bin One, is foundational content, or basic content that students need to understand and master if they truly are going to move to deeper and more complex cognitive tasks. At the core of the process is the belief that students can access the foundational content in Bin One at their own pace. Bin One is the content that we felt could be digitized in our learning management system.

It is important to note, once this is done, *it is done*. A tremendous amount of work has to be done upfront to prepare the material, tasks, mini-lessons and content for Bin One. Once this work is done, time becomes available to focus on opportunities for deeper learning. This is the promise of the responsive curriculum process. When done well, we can find time. Time is an elusive animal. Provide teams with time to focus on relationships, conferencing and deeper discussions in the classroom and everything improves in the learning ecosystem. Stay away from the technical jargon jungle. Keep it simple. Make it manageable. Start with the first unit. Design it, teach it, audit it, tweak it, memorialize it! A simple process, accelerated results.

A New Model for Curriculum Development

Phase 1 **Foundational Content (Digitized in LMS)**	*Phase 2* *Customized Curriculum & Deeper Learning (The Bullseye)*
Sequence of Topics	*Deep Learning Opportunity (DLO)*
Power content (Learning Targets)	*Project Based/Problem-Based Learning*
Academic Vocabulary	*Performance Tasks*
Supporting Text Sets	*Case Studies*
Mini-Lessons and Digital Resources	*Technical Literacy*
Practice for Mastery	

Our Keys:

- The need for new model aligns to our beliefs
- Collaboration is essential
- Connects to the vision

- Focus on impact
- Design for deep learning
- Commit to the responsive curriculum approach

The result of the work were model units, a coherent curriculum and deep professional discussions about instruction. The work continues. The cycle repeats, the opportunities to grow and get better are built into the work. Once the unit is created and the vision is emerging the next step is to look more closely at the classroom ecosystem. The next section brings us into the heart of it all, the learning environment. The purpose of creating an instructional vision, developing collaborative structures, and distributing leadership is so that ultimately the classroom is transformed. The next chapter looks at this more closely. Imagine what can happen when teams of educators make learning the driver. Imagine what can happen when we empower teams to change the nature of what happens in our classrooms.

Chapter Four Essential Questions:

- Is there a clear instructional and curriculum development vision in your school district?
- What work teams are in place to bring action to the vision?
- What curriculum work are you most proud of?
- What would change about the way you engage in curriculum work?
- Is there evidence of what is working and what is not working?
- What is the impact of your work?
- Is the curriculum adaptable and adjustable enough to change with the needs of students and changes in our world?
- Is professional collaboration rooted in the schools?
- Is deep learning at the core of curriculum work?
- Is there the will to commit to a responsive curriculum framework?

Spark Doing!

Below is a checklist summarizing the big ideas of this chapter into action steps that you may want to consider.

- Take the time to help the entire organization and stakeholders understand the instructional vision of your school district.
- Assess the current strengths and challenges of the existing curriculum development process.
- Evaluate the leadership structure and the capacity to design, implement, evaluate, modify and commit to a Responsive Curriculum Framework.
- Understand the degree to which your school district is a learning organization.
- Define, discuss and commit to the meaning of all students with intention and detail.
- Fully understand our proposed RCF and the tools used to organize content for the purpose of customizing deep learning.
- Invest time into the strategic formation of curriculum and instruction work teams.
- Establish the impact orientation focused on student outcomes.
- Follow through with the work of implementing a RCF while resisting the power of the status quo.
- Continuously reflect, analyze, evaluate, adjust and modify your work.
- Involve students in the process whenever possible.
- Celebrate short term and long-term wins.

Chapter Five

Instruction Reimagined: The Vision Realized

Imagine a place where the term "community of learners" was defined by inclusivity, diversity of thought and a multitude of gifts. Its space is saturated by a convergence of human, academic and intellectual resources from within and without. A place where students went to develop what they are good at and worried less about fixing what they are not good at.

By far, the most difficult thing to do in our profession is to change instructional practice. We have initiatives, jargon and terms for everything in education. What *we do not have* is a solid track record of real lasting change. This issue is personal to us. From this, a very simple idea was born. Could we create a learning system where the goal at every level was to always get better. In short, if we wanted to bring about real change the only way to succeed was to start in the classroom. Instruction, teaching and learning is the work. This has been and continues to be some of the most exciting, rewarding and complex work that we've encountered in our careers. What is offered in this chapter are lessons learned from real teachers in real classrooms. It is the shared expertise of some of the most talented educators around that have led to the blueprint provided in this chapter.

Every day, in hundreds of American classrooms, little faces are staring up at the adult that has been charged with taking care of academic and social-emotional needs. That responsibility is of utmost importance, and our *ability to respond* as educators, is a determining factor in helping to shape young lives for a very challenging world that awaits them.

Like you, our professional journey has taken many twists and turns. With each step along the way important guiding questions continue to fuel our need to keep learning about what makes our work so incredible. Over the years, we've found ourselves pondering these big questions. Does school have to sow the seeds of boredom? Should disengagement be the norm? Why aren't all students hungry to learn? Do students lose this yearning as they move through each grade? Can students at the end of formal education be just as fired up as an infant learning about the world for the first time? How do we create a classroom ecosystem where learning thrives? These questions continue to guide our thinking to this day and continue to fuel our ongoing professional learning.

Early on in our careers, we were not given the opportunity to wrestle with these questions. We were forced to attend professional development disguised as one day work sessions meant to transform our practice. The result of these "one hit wonder" professional development days was always the same, extreme fatigue, a yearning to get back with students and very little change. We can do better. *We must do better*. Every educator should be given the time, space and opportunity to articulate their driving professional questions and then study and explore them.

When you tie a core set of driving questions to everyday practice amazing things can happen. We will address professional learning later. First, time to dive into the idea of empowering teams across a system to create vibrant classroom ecosystems that are teaming with life. It can be done. We do it. And, more has to be done. It begins with the right teams, the right culture and most importantly a more responsive approach to our work. Static is out. Responsiveness is in. Organizations that learn this lesson will survive. Complexity is the new norm. We should embrace it, leverage it and unleash human potential. *This is what a real learning organization could be.*

Leveraging Teams to Change the Classroom

We live in complex times to say the least. Our access to information and how we live our lives has radically changed in just the last twenty years. Despite the rapid pace of change, for the most part, the American classroom has remained the same. Before we get too deep into this let us begin by acknowledging that it is not the fault of educators that things have not changed. I revere and admire the hard work that goes into making learning happen. This is not easy work. As a matter of fact, education in general is a complex endeavor. When you think about what goes into a typical day in a school the point quickly becomes clear.

Each day, millions of children, all from varying backgrounds, converge on American schools. The expectations and promises of school are simple, education is the path to prosperity in a democratic society. Given that technology provides access like no other time in human history, the importance of education becomes even more critical.

Today, the focus has to be on deep learning strategies for all students. Unleashing potential begins with focusing on creativity, critical thinking, communication, collaboration, literacy and performance tasks. The shift to a classroom that places the student at the center of the design is long overdue.

In education, the status quo and mediocrity are never enough. Our aim should always be to keep getting better. At minimum, we need to accept that we do not have all the answers. We can get better. Education and the American classroom as conceived centuries ago, should change to meet the demand of a new age. The lesson for leadership is this. Know your people. Meet them where they are at. Get out of the way of the willing, support the middle, and continue to listen carefully for the guardians of mediocrity.

Heads-up! Leaders, be cautious as to how much energy is put into directly addressing those who are defenders of the status quo. We have made this mistake and it is not worth the time! Address it, call it out, evaluate it and put your energy into those who want to grow and improve. The resistance becomes very uncomfortable with positive and inspiring growth when the forces of change momentum get rolling. Changing the classroom so that all students have a shot at success is urgent work. This work begins with the routines, habits and learning processes we embrace from day one.

It's time to give up control over planning for learning and begin to engage with students in designing instructional experiences. It's time to focus on building the relationships that support independence and ultimately interdependence. Now is our time. History is watching. A generation depends on us. We put our faith in educators, and place our trust in the classroom. It is after all, the epicenter and heart of our schools. Any change that doesn't start where instruction is delivered, does not offer hope for sustained transformation.

Any meaningful change begins by acting and taking risks. We can become our own worst nightmare. Paralyzed by inaction and always waiting for the best time to get going. Start somewhere. Begin the journey to changing the classroom equation. Begin the process of making school and every classroom a place of joy and lifelong learning. We ask ourselves at the end of each school year, were we the teachers and leaders, that one my students would want to become? Stop for a moment and ponder that. Would our students consider teaching as a profession because of us? Is our enthusiasm for the work infectious?

Taking the time to develop a clear set of guiding professional questions elevates the work. For us it is simple. Change the classroom ecosystem by changing the approach to how we conduct business. At this point, we will look more closely at how we change the equation from day one. The focus on agency, voice, autonomy and relationships is next. These kcy ingredients are the foundation for a successful environment where learning thrives.

Educators, this is our moment! Now is our time to build, from the ground up, a more humane school experience for our students. The focus of this part of the book is a blueprint to begin this work. Four key themes help to focus this section:

- Establishing a Culture of Learning
- Learning Routines and Habits in the Classroom
- The Learning Environment
- Innovative and Student-Centered Learning

Let's get to work.

Establishing a Culture of Learning

Having a voice matters. When we have a voice, we are engaged. When we have some freedom over how we will use time, we also are more likely to remain motivated and immersed in whatever we are working on. When you pair the voice and autonomy with caring relationships, the entire equation changes. Anything becomes possible. When we view our work in terms of these three variables, we approach classroom design from a completely different lens. The goal is not to put all of our energy into curating content with the hope of managing and controlling behaviors.

Transforming the classroom requires us to shift our focus. *Instead of focusing on compliance, control and management routines, focus on routines that provide agency, student voice, working together, autonomy and prioritize relationships.* When we put energy into developing a learning ecosystem anchored in these variables, not only will we create a more humane classroom that celebrates human potential, but the foundation for accelerated deep learning for all students will have been laid.

At this point, we have to pause and provide context and clarity. I can hear it right now. Many may be thinking "if I don't create order early on, if I don't establish routines, if I don't create and share rules, the year will be a giant headache." It is important to take on these core misconceptions directly. No change in practice will occur without first examining our current thinking, behaviors around opening a school year. The truth of the matter is that students will rise to any bar we set for them.

Each year millions of children go home for the summer. Without rigid structure and control they have the chance to engage in play, learn to use unstructured time, pursue topics of interest and use technology seamlessly. It is also important to note that the key to transforming our classrooms begins with creating a classroom community where students are involved from the very beginning in creating and developing the classroom expectations that will ultimately define the learning experiences.

Engaging students from day one in the classroom community provides a platform for engaging voices. Spending the opening of a school year working collaboratively, creatively and purposely in meaningful tasks that help frame the vision, beliefs and norms that will make the year a success, will pay off tenfold in February.

The critical question is how do we create a classroom that is focused on student voice, agency, autonomy and relationships? For those serious about changing the model of instruction and shifting to a thriving learning ecosystem, it is paramount to rethink the beginning of school. First, establishing high expectations, norms and routines is critical. The difference is subtle, but cannot be overlooked. This is not a teacher's task. *This is a classroom task.* It is about embracing a sense of purpose and community. From day one, commit to becoming a learning community.

Learning Routines and Habits in the Classroom

One critical mistake we make in school is that we rush to content or activities. We rush to fill time and get started on more important work out of fear that if we don't get started, we might run out of time. The first day of school is often about the rules, the syllabus, class overview, getting "to know you" activities and other opening of school rituals. The future classroom where students are truly developing the habits that cultivate lifelong learning begins with a slow, collaborative and deliberate commitment to co-creating the learning ecosystem. If we value it, if we model it, if we prioritize it, it will manifest.

The question becomes, what has to change?

The entire way we begin a new school year. Day one cannot look like it always has. We have to begin by working with our students to create a community of learners. Relationships have to be priority number one. So, in all practicality, what can be done? Begin by giving students a voice from the beginning with the creation of classroom learning expectations. For example:

- Engage students in meaningful reflection around the habits that lead to success
- Model the way learning will happen in your classroom from day one with this process
- Spend the first week on culture and team building
- Spend the first week modeling learning routines and expectations
- Worry less about content coverage
- Worry less about opening of school activities
- Engage students in meaningful reflection through writing

As we get deeper into this framework, we will discuss learning routines and habits in more detail. It cannot be stressed enough. Compliance is one way. Relationships and high expectations are another path. If we want to focus on learning and get closer to the environment where students are in control of their learning, we just can't skip this step. It is important to pause at this point and provide some important design considerations for practitioners to think about. In other words, what are explicit routines that can increase the likelihood that students will gain independence as learners? Some thoughts and examples will be explored next. Four essential areas need to be considered when starting this journey. Part Two tackles the learning environment.

The Learning Environment

When thinking about the learning environment and the routines that need to be established it helps to begin by thinking about four key areas:

- The focus on learning—understanding and developing learning plans
- Planning for learning—curating the resources necessary for students to master goals
- Managing learning and assessing progress
- Evidence of Learning

Helping Students Become More Self-Directed, Reflective and Focused on Their Own Learning.

Let's take a look at each of these important areas and tackle some big questions and considerations for teachers looking to transform the classroom. Again, *this is a process*. Intentional work early on with frequent tweaks leads to more student directed classroom ecosystems in the long run. Helping students develop the skills necessary to thrive in this environment takes time. It also will lead to the development of skills and habits that benefit us throughout our lifespan.

When looking to empower students to commit to directing their own learning, it is critical to begin by thinking about the following key questions:

- How will students develop the goals for learning? What routines need to be established to model this? How will you practice this early in a new school year?
- How will students personalize the key goals? How will you model this process early in a new school year?
- How will students develop a time management plan to work on the goals? When will this time exist? How will you model this process early in a new school year?

These questions are listed for a purpose. Prior to beginning a new school year, it is paramount to model for students the process of goal setting. This can be simple. One example where this was best illustrated, was a fourth-grade classroom. At the beginning of the school year the goal was to learn about what helps you as a learner. Students had the chance to address that goal. In doing so, the teacher had the chance to conference with students and let each of them personalize the goal based on the habits and areas they wanted to grow in.

This was deliberate and separate from content at first. After a couple rounds and practice the students began to apply this approach in ELA, math, science, social studies and most importantly to their independent study projects. Helping students set and personalize goals provides the fuel for autonomy and success in the classroom.

Unfortunately, we often skip this vital step.

Traditionally, we set the goal, provide the content, provide the practice, assess the content and move on. *This pattern may be part of the reason joy slowly erodes for learning.* We can disrupt it. Be intentional about goals and the routines associated from day one.

Intentionally Planning for Learning in a Self-Directed, Reflective Environment

The second question is equally important, how do we intentionally plan for learning in this environment? As a disclaimer, this is hard to do and requires a lot of time upfront, before learning. The good news is this, once the key framework is created it gets easier the second, third and fourth time you use it. The key takeaway is this. Invest time upfront to get this part right so that in the future tweaking, enhancements and innovation are the drivers of improvement, not planning.

In order to get started thinking about developing a platform for students to access content some key questions to get started include:

- What resources will I make available for my students? How will I help students find and review those resources?
- How will I help my students go deeper into their learning and acquire more knowledge?
- How will I organize the resources and how will I model for students how to find the resources and negotiate the environment?

These are all critical questions. When thinking about letting students "loose" into the wild, it is important to assure that the unit of instruction they are accessing is well designed. Spending time creating a structure for students to access resources and content is important. The best version is a unit that has everything a student will need to get started from the beginning. Helping students learn how to set goals, manage time, and then access resources early on is important. This naturally leads to question three. How do we help students manage and direct their own learning?

Helping Students Manage and Direct Their Learning

Once we have established learning routines, helped students understand learning expectations, and empowered them to personalize goals, the next step is teaching them time management. This is an important step. Students are told at every second in school what to do, how to do it and how long they have to do it. We rarely take the time to model and practice how to take a large task, break it down and plan to complete it.

In other words, teaching and modeling time management is a critical life skill. All successful classrooms make this a priority. Assuming students will know what to do, how to do it, how long it will take or even where to get started will lead to teacher frustration. Be intentional early on about modeling practices. Below are some key questions to get started thinking about helping students direct their own learning:

- What tools can you develop to help students prioritize tasks and establish a work plan?
- What opportunities do students have to talk about the plan with you? How will feedback be given?
- What tools can be provided to help students when they are stuck? Struggling?
- How often do students revisit their plan?

There are many examples of what this might look like. Providing you the magic answer is not the intention of this book. There is no one best prototype. The best approach is to engage the team in designing the first attempt at a time management/pacing tool. Try it out, then learn from what works. Tweak the tool. Repeat. The best examples we have seen were the result of action research. It is important to note that one of the key components of a successful learning environment is the presence of a tool. Generally speaking:

- Establish a routine for having students work on this plan.
- Set goals and personalize goals.
- Identify tasks, workflow.

- Provide an opportunity for students to determine what they will work on and how long it might take given the time constraints.
- Provide frequent opportunities for teacher and student conferences (in groups or individually) to reflect on the plan, progress and problems.

Before we roll into the final question, there is another question that often comes up when we talk about creating a self-directed classroom. What is the teacher doing if students are all working? Rest assured, there is plenty to do! What we have found is that teachers have more time to build relationships, assess student understanding, lead mini-lessons and conference with students. The result turns out to be, more engagement and improved outcomes and a teacher that is far more satisfied with this work than once was imaginable. Don't believe us? Try it for yourself. Again, it's subtle but the point of this final section is this, where does the ownership for this fall? If you have been thinking about this, your answer would be, the student of course.

Helping Students Produce Evidence of Learning

Once you have goals, a student learning plan, learning routines in place you might be ready to take it to the next level and ask, how will my students produce evidence that they have learned? The normal tools may still apply. Keep using them. If you want to take it to the next level, consider these points and questions:

- Ask students in the learning plan to provide a process for how they will demonstrate their mastery.
- Provide the opportunity to conference with students and let them prove they have learned.
- Let students reflect on the learning process and identify the habits that they are good at, and areas they need to continue to work at in the next unit.
- Do students have an opportunity to innovate or do something authentic with their work? If so, who is the audience for this?

The final part is intended to tie this all together and provide an example of what this might look like for those getting started all the way to the most extreme version. We've had the pleasure to see both ends of this spectrum at work and everything in between. The key, let teams go in the sandbox. Keep the instructional vision out front. Look for outcomes, learn along the way!

Innovative and Student-Centered Learning

The whole point of this section is to get back to the central premise of this book. How do we create systems and collaborative teams all around an instructional vision that ultimately creates classrooms where student learning thrives? As you have seen, the steps may seem intuitive but the larger goal remains, all students deserve to learn in this environment. This brings us full circle to the importance of getting all of the other key parts to this work in place. You can't rush, but if you do happen to find yourself in a place where the alignment is lacking, you can still make a difference.

Innovative and student-centered learning environments are not new. Their execution and seeing this concept in practice is as elusive as Bigfoot and as rare as a unicorn. We can do better. We should all be working to assure that as students go through school their curiosity, creativity, ability to critically think, communicate, collaborate and problem solve only improves. Instead, we all too often see the opposite. The challenge is simple, be the difference maker today for students.

Simple shifts in thinking can yield great results. The following are reflective questions to be continuously asked:

- Is my classroom (or are the classrooms in my district building) more teacher centered or student-centered? How do I know?
- Does the culture support innovation, risk taking and action research?

Ask the above big questions. Then go on a scavenger hunt and look for evidence. The personal audit of an instructional vision can be the beginning of real change. Build on what you see, plant seeds where it doesn't exist, reexamine practices at every level (district, building, classroom) and begin the journey towards rethinking the classroom experience.

Chapter Five Essential Questions:

- Do classroom practices reflect the instructional vision?
- Do change and improvement initiatives focus on instruction?
- What educational purposes fuel the staff in wanting to get better?
- Does every staff member have the opportunity to think deeply about the educational questions most important to them?
- What are the core set of driving instructional questions with which all must wrestle?
- Do the classroom ecosystems reflect the instructional vision of the district?
- Is there more time spent on control over planning or on designing instructional experiences?
- Does maintaining compliance receive more attention than the learning ecosystem?
- Are the instructional development processes static or responsive?

Spark Doing!

Below is a checklist summarizing the big ideas of this chapter into action steps that you may want to consider.

- Conduct thorough research on best instructional practices that put students at the center of the teaching and learning ecosystem.
- Communicate a clear instructional vision.
- Communicate the Whys for changing and/or improving instructional practices.
- Discuss and answer the essential core questions driving instructional decisions and practices.
- Create a systemic culture of supporting instructional innovations by providing aligned goals, professional learning, resources, encouragement and celebrations.
- Organize and leverage teams of district administrators, principals, teachers, staff and students to begin changing and/or improving classroom learning environments.
- Focus on defining and embedding the practices of student agency, voice, autonomy, outcomes and relationships.
- Focus on defining and implementing learning routines and habits of mind that become the foundation of a student-centered learning ecosystem.
- Focus on and implement instructional practices that develop reflective and self-directed skills in students grounded in evidence of learning.

Chapter Six

Personalized Professional Learning:
A Blueprint for Getting Started

Imagine a place where the pervasive discourse of the day among talented professionals had an inspirational and inviting quality to it. Its evolution is rooted in research, risk, relationships and reflection. A place where autonomy and collaboration were not clichés but necessary to upholding the brilliance of professional human practice—unreplaceable by machine or model. A place without locked doors and papered windows. Its conventions are not shackled by accountabilities created by those with no sensibilities.

When was the last time you learned something?

This question can hit you hard if you stop and truly reflect on the last time you voluntarily chose to learn something new. Even more sobering, when was the last time you learned something deeply? The purpose of professional learning is simple, we should always aim to grow professionally. The ultimate goal is to make the vision become reality. We have argued that building collaborative teams is the path to improving the likelihood that this outcome can be achieved. Given this premise, it should not be a surprise that the notion of professional learning needs to be retooled as well.

At the heart of professional learning is teacher leadership and opportunities to grow. Empowering teams of teachers to showcase and share expertise is a sure path to improving teacher practice. Professional learning cannot be something done to educators, it has to be *something done with them*. The following beliefs begin to frame concrete steps school districts can take, to begin to build a more robust and impactful system rooted in ongoing professional learning.

Consider these big ideas:

- Distinguish between training and professional learning.
- Organize professional learning around priorities.
- Make professional learning about design work.
- Spark doing through action research and responsive professional learning cycles.

Distinguishing Between Training and Professional Learning

This sounds simple and almost intuitive. The dissatisfaction with professional learning stems from a perceived lack of relevance and all too often a top-down approach where everyone is subjected to the same learning. This entire book has been about personalization, building structures to collaborate, and creating classrooms where student learning is the focus. Professional learning needs to also reflect this reality. The fundamental unit of the school community is the team. One of the most important things leaders can do is spend time thinking about these three crucial questions:

- What teams exist within a building?
- How healthy and vibrant are those teams?
- What teams need to be created to help advance the vision and mission?

Once these questions have been answered it is time to begin reflecting on professional learning. For the practitioner, supporting teams with a personalized approach to professional growth is the only way to move the needle and impact organizational culture.

Consider the following:

Identify required training that all employees need and call it what it is, *training*. Do not confuse what has to be done with the opportunity to provide targeted professional learning based on the needs of each team. For example, if you purchase a new student management system and everyone needs to learn about it for a system wide application, call it training, schedule it, provide it, follow up on it and move on. Once you know what required training needs to be provided you can begin to focus on a bigger conversation, creating a system where meaningful professional learning is not only the norm, but the expectation. This distinction provides an opportunity to keep the vision out front.

This shift can translate into a significant opportunity to frame the conversation around why professional learning and the time we devote to it is critical for our profession. We have to create a sense of urgency *around the why*. If we leave this to chance, confuse these constructs or force adults to all learn the same thing in the name of growth and professional development expect more of the same. Avoiding the same old results requires assembling an innovative team of leaders and teachers willing to rethink and reinvigorate professional learning aligned with the instructional vision and improvement goals.

Perhaps this is best illustrated with an example. Several years ago, while working in a rather large district (not the district referred to frequently in the book) we had the privilege of serving on the district professional development committee. From the beginning, something didn't feel right. The committee, with all good intentions, committed to providing the entire district professional development on note taking. Again, the intention was good. Note taking is a solid instructional strategy. The problem, on scale, not every employee or stakeholder needed to learn about note taking, nor was it relevant. How did note taking help advance the why? How did note taking remind and reconnect teams back to the why?

The obvious answer, it didn't.

The approach of one universal theme and with standard professional learning was top down and destined for failure. As an aside, you know what this particular district does not do well today? You guessed it, note taking. This brings us full circle. Start with the required training, make it clear why everyone needs this and then begin leveraging the power of teams. As a building level leader, ask:

- What is our vision?
- Where are we going?
- Do you believe in this direction?
- What do you need this year?
- What goals does your team have?
- How can we support those goals with meaningful professional learning?
- How will it impact instruction, say, tomorrow?

When we embed ourselves at the team level, we get closer to the heart of it all, which is the classroom. The classroom is where the magic happens. Real change, lasting change, cultural change, only happens, when we impact instruction. Never be afraid to take it to the street level, listen, reflect and empower. When we do, lasting change begins to take shape.

What then is the key shift in practice? Move away from doing professional learning to people towards a model that commits to learning *with* people! At first this can be overwhelming; it may even sound like The Wild West! This is not the intention. You can have choice and voice in professional learning, with some constraints that help focus the work. Read on to find out more!

Professional Learning and Priorities

A natural starting point for moving to a more personalized approach to professional learning is to introduce the concept of "bounded choice." Bounded choice allows a school district or any organization to identify themes and priority focus areas that provide stakeholders with the opportunity to align their professional learning time to what they might need. This is a natural starting point in the evolution of a more personalized professional development approach. Bounded choice or a menu approach is the opportunity for teacher teams to sign up for professional development or learning that is more aligned to the particular needs of their team. Where should you begin?

First, start by identifying the core academic and instructional priorities for the organization. Call this road map the one-year instructional plan. The best plans are based on the vision, clarify the mission and are tied to outcomes. Consider the following:

- Meet with each building team.
- Reflect on a bold and aggressive one year plan by identifying key themes/areas of learning.
- Clarify the mission.
- Set the short-term goals/priorities.
- Seek to determine success criteria, how will you know you are moving?

Next, work to find teachers, administrators and teams in each building that would be willing to showcase and share their expertise. As noted earlier, the Instructional Leadership Team (ILT) is a natural starting place once established. The ILT should be a broad reflection of the teams within the organization and be a way to lead this important work.

Finally, engage teams and provide the opportunity for them to sign up to learn from their colleagues on scheduled professional learning days. As you begin to march down this path, know that it may take several iterations before it becomes automated, systemic and the norm. There are two key takeaways questions to ask depending on the goals and priorities:

Should the teachers and team members be from the same content background?

Should the teachers and team members be from across grade level, building or the organization?

The answer to the questions above depends a lot on the overall objective. For instance, if you are looking to shore up the quality of programming and articulate across content areas, having all the science teachers get together makes sense. However, if you really want to talk about instruction and transforming instructional practice. Consider mixing the groups. We have seen the power of creating professional learning teams that span every level, building and subject area. If you add classified and paraprofessionals to this mix the result is a power team, posed to learn and ultimately impact student learning.

Imagine what could happen when kindergarten teachers are in the same room as high school teachers. The result, often, is deep, meaningful, purposeful conversations about instruction, teaching, and student learning. This is the sweet spot. Imagine the power of that conversation! If you want students to improve their reading and writing in high school, ask a primary teacher!

Over the years, when teacher teams get out of their silos and talk with professionals about instruction, amazing things begin to happen around the entire system. Further, when cross group different grade levels begin conversations about the vision, the entire system begins to move. This is the desired outcome. When the whole system is moving and focused on the whole child and their learning, all students win.

Develop a core group of Professional Learning leaders from every level. Organize this team around the themes, vision and priorities. Keep it focused on instruction (not curriculum or tools) and give people choice. Imagine a professional learning day where teams of educators from every level gather together and get to talk about how their collective impact improves student learning. Imagine when primary teachers have an opportunity to learn about rigor, deeper learning from high school teachers. The synergy across an entire district can be unleashed.

Designing Professional Learning

The goal remains the same. Improve student outcomes for all learners.

There is a second kind of professional learning that is less planned and less systemic. This second kind of professional learning is job embedded and involves instructional design. When teams design instructional prototypes together, teach them, reflect together on them, tweak them and do this repeatedly, everything gets better.

The best professional learning is useful to educators the next day. When educators learn something, it is important for them to put it into practice. The sooner, the better. All too often professional learning is not impactful because too much time passes between what was learned and implementation.

Imagine that a team of educators are given time to design a unit of instruction together, offer feedback, incorporate more hands-on and project-based aspects to the unit and then are ready to go use it when they start the next unit. This is the type of impact that can improve outcomes. This is the essence of the action research and responsive learning cycle. In education we love acronyms, so we'll give you another one: *The RLC*. Let's dive into this concept a bit.

Action Research and Responsive Learning Cycle (RLC)

Does the professional learning time spark hands on doing? This is the essential question for any meaningful professional learning. In other words, do educators feel empowered to impact students' learning? Further, is there a way for ideas to germinate? Innovation without an outlet can create pockets of excellence. Any district or organization looking to stimulate and foster deeper learning needs to provide a process or outlet for teams to gather, design, research, evaluate and then tweak.

One systematic way to act is to embrace the concept of the RLC. The Responsive Learning Cycle is a process and protocol driven experience that tends to favor creative design and less controlled and contrived lesson curation. The focus is always the unit level. When you think in terms of units of instruction you are thinking about a time interval of 3–6 weeks. This provides enough time for the cycle to work and be interactive. It also provides and preserves the art of the day-to-day teaching that happens in a classroom. We design in teams at the unit level for maximum impact.

What might this look like?

- Focus on a grade level team.
- Empower them to design their next unit together.
- Have them teach the unit.
- Audit for impact and alignment.
- Reflect, adjust and redo.

The key to success is the conversation. When teachers are reflecting on practice before, during and after instruction the potential impact is magnified. This is the sweet spot for professional learning! We want all professionals spending every minute we have talking and acting on the heart of where the magic happens. Professional learning focused on the classroom level that empowers teachers through meaningful design and dialogue provides a blueprint for elevating our profession.

Chapter Six Essential Questions:

- How deeply rooted is professional learning (PL) in your culture? Are PL activities energizing, renewing, collaborative and require reflection and action?
- How do you distinguish between training and learning?
- How does staff feel about your professional learning model? Is staff involved in designing PL?
- Are PL activities aligned with the visions and goals of the district?
- Are PL activities tailored to school building, grade level, program and individual staff needs?
- How is PL built into the performance evaluation system? Are staff accountable to one another for growth, encouragement and support? Is there a feeling of bounded choice?
- How do you assess the effectiveness of your PL program?

Spark Doing!

Below is a checklist summarizing the big ideas of this chapter into action steps that you may want to consider.

- Organize priorities aligned to the vision before school starts.
- Asses the professional learning needs of all staff.
- Identify teachers' leaders, administrative leaders, outside experts that can help lead the breakout work.
- Schedule the PL days ahead of time and allow teams/ individuals to sign up to areas of relevance to their work.

- Allow for time within the PL time for teams to process what they learned, and design something they can use the next time they are working with students.
- Celebrate success and professionalism.

Chapter Seven

Think This Not That:
More Stories from the Journey

Imagine a place where the customs and constrictions of time were not enemies of learning but instead, allies of learning. Where the barriers of 50-minute seat time within 175 days did not exist. A milieu infused with the opportunity to learn almost anything—anywhere—anytime—and at any pace. Where mastery and understanding were conquerable for all. A place that does not subscribe to the doctrine of the achievement bell curve.

The purpose of this chapter is to highlight a few stories that showcase the principles, ideas and practices shared throughout this book. More importantly, we want to showcase that transformation is possible, and that learning from one another results in extraordinary growth that ultimately benefits students. You're about to read about an innovative program that transforms the high school experience, how a team of teachers reimagined the elective experience in middle school and how a small change in an elementary school transformed what we thought kids could achieve. Each example draws on the big ideas discussed throughout this book.

End of the Line for the High School Factory Model

At Mayfield High School, a dedicated and talented team of educators used the model of professional learning detailed above and went to work. They took an idea and belief and used it to impact student learning. There is power in unleashing a team that is passionate about a big sticky educational problem. The problem is as old as our profession. How do you move from a one size fits all, industrial model of school, to a more personalized, student-centered system? It begins with the right team and the willingness to do something different and possibly fail.

How do you change the entire essence of the high school factory model? This was the fundamental question with which a wise administrative team had to wrestle. The answer, develop a small team of eager and willing faculty and let them loose. The challenge, build a program so irresistible that students would flock to the program and sign up. Coaching this team through this process was one of the most fascinating and rewarding professional experiences of which we've had the pleasure to be part. Instead of imposing top-down change on an entire staff we empowered the few and intrigued the many.

Seven teachers, off site, took time to build what ultimately would become the Option Program. A completely self-paced, structured and supported learning experience with a capstone project embedded into the school day. Even better, in year one, just under half of the senior class chose to be part of this option. Fast forward to the present day and the program is now a comprehensive option for students in grades 9–12.

The keys to designing and implementing the Option Program were the following:

- Identifying the needs by asking people, what could school be?
- Identifying space to begin launching a program.
- Approval and buy in from the core team (district, building, teacher team and Board.)
- Identifying the staff.
- Recruiting the students.
- Branding the work and model.
- Scheduling the students.
- Providing Professional learning to the teacher team (this is a sizable commitment to get it right.)

- Soliciting constant feedback and readjustment.
- Minding the outcomes and maintaining rigor in the core curriculum.

Electrifying the Elective Wheel

It was a quiet Friday afternoon after a long week of teaching, learning and leading. Nothing beats the "quiet Friday" in education. It's a rare gem. I remember this day because I felt the need to get up, walk across campus to the Middle School and call a meeting with the administrative team. For years, I had been bothered by the "elective wheel" we used at our middle school. Even before the push to personalize and think about deep learning, the idea that anything good could happen during a condensed six-week rotation where students were bombarded with stuff did not sit well.

The meeting was odd. I remember walking in, and beginning by saying, "We need to change the elective wheel for next year. It just doesn't work anymore." Looking back, all three of the administrators in the room were perplexed. This confusion moved to a defensive posture and eventually a rather spirited conversation. Do not lose sight of what is going on here. It is 2:00 p.m. on a Friday afternoon in a middle school. Victory was close, and this guy Dr. Kelly, from the central office showed up with a crazy idea. Let's be bold and break the model that has ruled the middle level since the 1970s! After about 30 minutes I left.

On Monday, after a weekend to ponder the request, the team had warmed to the idea. With support, the vision, mission and a reminder of the importance of deeper learning for all students the Our House Circuits were born! The circuits at the middle school reflected a sketch of a deeper learning, more authentic, more student driven experience. Their first concept was a homerun. It checked all of the boxes. Why teach digital media productions, art and STEM as separate "topics?" Why not bundle these disciplines into one, call it a circuit, teach kids the skills they need and let them lose on big, sticky real problems!

Thus, the circuits were born!

They continue to evolve. We have added a social-emotional learning circuit, wellness circuit and continue to innovate and iterate. Project and problem-based learning became the cornerstone approach to learning. It's about skills and foundational content and how it is fused with the competencies we as a district identified as necessary for life after school. I want to commend the middle school team for their bold action around this idea. It was after all a Friday at 2:00 p.m. Most would have checked out. Not this team. The result, cultural change. I am sure they are not done either. THEY KEEP ROLLING!

Talent and Passion Never Truly Retires

A mentor and perhaps one of the most inspirational teachers I have had the pleasure to learn with showed me the importance of creating a learning culture, firsthand. After thirty-five years Mrs. Jean Uthe retired. However, she wasn't done! Her expertise, knowledge, commitment and passion for teaching and learning was going to be leveraged one more time!

It was a cold October day by Cleveland standards (and the weather typically is hit or miss here). I remember sitting with the leadership team wrestling with a staffing problem. We had steadily seen an increase in enrollment in one grade level, at one building. It was October. Creating another classroom section and moving kids from their teacher and friends at this time of year did not make sense. Was there another solution?

The team settled on a bold idea. Let's bring back one of our retired, innovative, veteran teachers and let her lose to create the most personalized classroom she could imagine. *The Innovation Lab was born!* Over the course of the year a cohort of students would spend a quarter of the school year in this room learning in a completely different format.

In many ways, the environment modeled and reflected the Option Program at the high school where students had the chance to customize and personalize their school day. What I witnessed during the evolution of this experience was nothing short of incredible. Students came out of their shell and focused on developing critical thinking habits of mind. They moved through content at a pace appropriate for them and had the chance to engage in a capstone project.

The capstone project that is infused in this program is not like anything we had ever seen done before. Students, in our upper elementary level, were engaged in authentic, deep and rigorous study. From the topics they chose, to the depth of their understanding was nothing short of incredible. I remember seeing students (that struggled academically) shine during this experience. I watched struggling learners polish their research skills, comprehension skills, writing skills and truly flourish as learners. Behavior incidents in this environment plummeted and student engagement soared.

This would not have been possible unless Ms. Uthe was willing to say *yes*. To suspend "retirement" and step out of the box and back into the arena. The lessons learned; professional conversations that were had set the stage. The passion and ability to sketch up a prototype for future transformation was born from this classroom.

As a result, our Synergy Program was developed. On the heels of a global pandemic in 2021 we launched a brand-new elective experience for ALL of our elementary students. Now, each week our students have the opportunity to begin developing the habits of mind and skills that will be necessary for deep learning and future work at the middle and high school level.

It was an idea that was born out of a problem. It defied conventional wisdom and followed the blueprint offered in this book. Followed the blueprint in this book. It unleashed a movement in elementary schools across the district. I remain inspired by Ms. Uthe and her contribution to moving the needle and changing the culture.

Lincoln or Bust!

Doris Kearns Goodwin quoted President Lincoln in her unparalleled work about Lincoln's leadership and that of his cabinet team in the book, *Team of Rivals*.

"No man resolved to make the most of himself, can spare time for personal contention. Still less can he afford to take all the consequences, including the vitiating of his temper, and the loss of self-control. Yield larger things to which you can show no more than equal right; and yield lesser ones, though clearly your own. Better give your path to a dog, than be bitten by him in contesting for the right. Even killing the dog would not cure the bite."

What we can take from this masterful quote by our 16th president, is not to compare ourselves to Lincoln and his cabinet but instead to simply illustrate the point that acting on a vision for the purposes of improvement and transformation can only be done by highly motivated, strong willed, compassionate and passionate people. We mentioned that our cabinet team is feisty. They are also brilliant and highly motivated, sometimes causing a digression into tunneled vision debates and spirited arguments.

My predecessor, a brilliant superintendent, politician and leader in his own right, adorned the cabinet room with a painting of President Lincoln's cabinet over a mantle, giving the room a feeling of statesmanship and governance. The room also includes a life size bust of President Lincoln. The painting has since been replaced by an interactive flatscreen but the bust of Lincoln remains.

At one of our meetings early on in my tenure, the cabinet team was exceptionally stressed and emotions were running high over the many issues associated with staffing. Parents wanted teachers added to various grade levels in a couple of our elementary schools and made their voices heard. The school tax levy vote was right around the corner. The staffing budget was stretched. The unions were worried about class sizes going up. The work to transform our district was exciting and producing great results. But the stress on our team mounted as we addressed the issues of making a vision a reality. The financial and human costs of change are tricky and managing them often brings out our best but sometimes also brings out high levels of frustration.

Being able to walk in the shoes of another (as Lincoln so often did with tremendous empathy and emotional intelligence) is the only way to put ego aside and clear one's mind in order to see a clear path forward.

A lack of empathy is destructive to a team. I was listening to a particular debate on a highly sensitive issue. It was starting to get very tense. Some were starting to withdraw to their own strong-willed silos of protection. I too was getting the urge to force my case and pull rank when I found myself looking at the Lincoln bust. Not to reduce the wise greatness of man such as President Lincoln, but I found myself in a Charlie Brown moment. You know, the moment when all he hears from Lucy is *wah wah wha*! So, I stood up, grabbed the bust of Lincoln and placed it on the table directly in front of my most animated teammate. Respectfully, and with a smile on my face, I described what Lincoln stood for as a leader.

The sheer act of getting up and placing the bust on the table took the tension out of the room. Fortunately, all of my colleagues like to laugh and can be self-deprecating. We all laughed, got back to work and solved the problem by considering each other's needs and wants.

Needless to say, using the Lincoln bust became a routine when someone was going off the deep end. It became so effective, that some would award the bust to themselves in the middle of a conversation. Sometimes we would even vote on who earned the Lincoln award at the end of a meeting. That bronze bust of "Honest Abe" became something that represented what we truly valued and loved about one another.

The Pencil and the Epiphany

Throughout this book we have discussed our moments of making our vision become reality. And how, these moments of transformation are deeply meaningful. Cultivating the soil to grow the vision took time and support from our terrific board of education, school community, students and administrative team. The use of technology as an instructional tool was one of the keys to our transformation.

Wireless infrastructure, one-to-one learning devices, digital learning management systems, digitized curriculum, digital learning tools and the professional learning to go with these technologies did not exist in our school system when we first designed our actionable vision.

In working with the school board to explain the whys, learning benefits and costs of moving forward with technology there was a healthy skepticism from board members. When thinking about what may add perspective to the board's thinking we realized that a national and global view of educational research and trends were needed. So, to that end, we decided to forgo the state conference and attend the Model Schools Conference with the school board and a team of building administrators.

The Model Schools Conference presents schools around the world that are transforming the way students are learning based on research about instructional engagement, success in school and skills needed to compete for jobs in a global economy. It was a lot to take in for anyone who did not view education from outside the walls of their own schools.

We as a team met in the evening after the first day of sessions to discuss what we learned and what we had observed. We had a great time discussing and debating. But make no mistake, there were many tough questions and many eye-opening moments as we attempted to relate what we were learning to our own situation.

We discussed budgetary impacts, professional learning strategies, community acceptance, the difficulties of change and union concerns. Most interestingly, there were questions about what students might do with access to personal learning devices. Would students use Chromebooks for what was intended or would it cause more problems than it was worth? Cheating, accessing inappropriate sites, plagiarism, sharing of information, helping each other solve problems and test security among others, were all concerns.

One board member in particular (who is a great guy, a community gem and a trusted leader for more than twenty years) was still not convinced of our plan to improve instruction by providing every student with a laptop. He just didn't see technology as a learning tool and was not sure of the return on the investment. He questioned the innovation of digital tools for learning and I am sure he was speaking for many others. This particular board member had attended our schools and lived in the community all of his life. He knew hundreds of successful, motivated and accomplished people of good character from our school system.

What is wrong with memorization? What is wrong with paper and pencil? It has been that way for years. Can students really learn without textbooks? His questioning and skepticism would prove to be valuable because it foreshadowed what we as a leadership team would face as we moved forward. Being a critical theorist was clearly his genius.

The next day, I woke up wondering if attending this conference would result in anything tangible. Would it be more than a great time bonding and building our relationships? Would it inspire us or scare us back into status quo thinking?

We all attended a packed general session on the next day. I don't recall the speaker and the exact details of the information and stories presented. But I do remember the looks on the faces of the board and the administrative team when the case was being made that the skill of memorization was not enough for success in our world given that information is ubiquitous and at our fingertips.

The message was starting to slowly sink in. Then came the epiphany!

A simple and relatable story about one of the most educational and innovative tools ever invented—THE PENCIL! Suddenly we all understood. The pencil, while around for decades, was also invented. In fact, teachers in the 1800's worried what students would do with the pencil. Would they use it for the intended purposes? Would they poke each other with it? Would they write inappropriate messages to each other? Would they write on the desks and ruin them? Would the teacher lose control if students would rather write something down than memorize it? We got it! Change is inevitable and will always be hard!

We understood that the point of this story was not about the tool itself, it was about the importance of innovation matching the needs of the learner and what the world requires of our students when they leave us.

The pencil story was never forgotten by the team. It was retold time and time again as we reminded ourselves about our purpose. As for the board member particular to this story who was asking what many others wanted to know, well, he became one of the biggest advocates for our plan to use technology as a tool for transforming instruction. He helped hundreds of our entrenched community members see the *whys* and the logic for the investment. All of the board members did! And, each have their own story about becoming champions for transformation.

Thanks to our school board, there is a hidden lesson here for all leaders, administrators and board members alike. Leadership takes knowing who you are and what you believe in. It takes a steadfast commitment to community values and the individuals we serve. It takes courageous people willing to stand on the island of change. We all know this, but of course, it's easier said than done. The lesson learned from our school board is that traditional values and practices can work in concert with visions and dreams. One informs the other. One allows the other. Plowing forward without intertwining tradition and visionary goals impedes the path forward.

You Know What Assume Means!

Students and their learning need to be at the center of our work. Students also need to be involved in our work. They bring incredible surprising insights and realism to the table. As we have mentioned throughout this book, we involve students in all kinds of meaningful professional committee work. They interact with teachers, staff, administrators, board members, mayors, chiefs and lawmakers. Telling the story above reminds us of a simple yet powerful moment that brought forward a realization that no staff member or leader thought to discuss because of our assumptions about young people.

Once, we were talking with our student advisory council while eating pizza. We were discussing the purposes of going one to one with Chromebooks. Students provided meaningful insight into the possible uses and how instruction as well as engagement in learning might be enhanced. They also provided insight into our readiness and what would need to be done. They were concerned that some teachers were more ready than others and the Chromebooks would just become a fancy worksheet.

From that discussion came the insight that we adults assume that all students, because of their ages, are tech savvy. A sophomore in the group spoke up and said, *"You know Dr. Kelly, just because I am sixteen doesn't mean that I am a digital native as all of you adults assume."* It made me stop and think. I asked him to explain. I was having a hard time conceptualizing what he meant. He told the story of his younger sister getting an iPad when she was just four years old—something he didn't get when he was four. He went on to explain that there are generational differences among students in school and students within the same family.

The point he was making was that assuming all students were digital natives and using technology is a bad assumption. It was pointed out that just because students knew how to use the digital tools of social media did not mean they would be eager to use digital devices when learning. Students also questioned if we had considered the issues of access, equity and use as it pertained to students of poverty.

Powerful conversation!

Just as we had discussed the readiness of staff, we now needed to discuss the readiness levels of students. I brought these student insights back to the administrative team and as a result we continued to examine our policies, practices, professional learning, rollouts and use of Chromebooks through the lenses of students.

The leadership lesson learned was one of not getting caught up in the glitz, glam and excitement of the initiative. It reminded us of the importance of research, thinking deeply and gaining stakeholder perspective.

Think Purpose not Politics

Change for change's sake is an overused expression by those who resist, often driving leaders to a place my friend and colleague, Frank Forsthoefel, called a "regression to the mean." Frank is another highly intuitive leader who taught me the power of thinking beneath the program policy proposals in order to understand if the proposed change will honor the purpose. Honoring the purpose, is in our opinion, the most important expression that leaders can use to both inspire others toward growth and rebuff the cries of change for change's sake.

There was much discussion and change in instructional practices evolving at our high school regarding in-depth learning and student ownership of learning. There was plenty of resistance among particular pockets of staff but there was also considerable desire and momentum in moving away from the instructional routines of lecture, memorization and regurgitation.

One such desire was a teacher led committee to move from the traditional forty-five-minute period to some form of block scheduling. Block scheduling had been a successful program policy for many high schools across the nation as long as there was an investment in aligning professional learning with teaching in a block schedule.

I have been a proponent of block scheduling for many years. In fact, I did my doctoral research on the topic and led a high school of thirty-five hundred students to a block schedule that is still in place twenty-five years later. That change met many of our goals and students do benefit but the question of time and learning and the purpose of structured schedules have haunted me for many years.

Let me be clear about the difficulty I encountered, a quarter of a century ago, in moving to a block schedule. It was brutal, with intense criticism and calls for my dismissal as the associate principal. So, when our current principal came to us and suggested block scheduling, the hairs stood up on the back of my neck. Did I want to relive the intense criticism of this kind of change as a superintendent while dealing with the vitriol of a pandemic? No bleeping way!

However, the principal and his committee made up of students and staff continued to research the pros and cons. The committee was becoming more convinced that the positive impact a change to block scheduling could have on student-teacher relationships, discipline, planning periods, stress, lunch schedules, hallway disruptions and clubs was worth the change.

The principal Jeff Legan, one of the best I have known, came to us with a proposal. I hesitated. My fear, however, had been overridden by my question about purpose. The committee's research and reasoning were sound. Their hearts and minds were in it. They were ready to take a risk and help promote the change. I did not shut them down but wanted time to think about it.

There was a deeper purpose that needed to be explored.

The issue of time and learning and how it can help or hinder the learner had to be investigated on a much deeper level. So, I turned to my colleague and co-author of this book Dr. Patrick Ward. We sat in Dr. Ward's office asking deeper questions about scheduling. We understood the mechanical benefits and knew there would be instructional benefits with the right professional learning. However, the driving impacts of time on learning and learning on time nagged us. We just couldn't support a major policy change without taking a more meaningful shot at solving the time and learning issue. And, as a superintendent I also wasn't ready to use up a good deal of political trust and capital to make this change. After several conversations we eventually came to the issues of agency, engagement, outcomes and opportunity and how to infuse more of these principles into the teaching and learning process.

We met with Principal Legan to explain our position. He was disappointed at first but as we talked, I could see the wheels in his head turning. The recognized Ohio Principal of the Year then had the courage to go back to his committee and turn the entire conversation on its ear. To the credit of the teachers and students they dug in and began considering and discussing the deeper issues.

In the meantime, I contacted a friend and colleague, Doug Mader, who is a true visionary with incredible people skills, drive and intellect, and served in another extraordinary and high performing school district. Turns out he and his team got the go ahead to design a program that attempted to address the issues of time and learning while enhancing rigor and ownership of learning.

When we took our committee to visit, their program had been in place for a year. Our committee returned to Mayfield on fire! They got right to work creating and designing. What they came up with was remarkable. They called it the *Option Program*. A program open to all students in grades 9–12. It breaks down the barriers of time and learning and is grounded in rigorous content, project/problem-based learning and infuses the principles of agency, engagement, outcomes and opportunity. We were so impressed with the design of the Option Program we decided to redesign space to match the kinds of teaching and learning that would take place. The staff and the kids love it. The middle school leadership and teacher teams also began infusing the principles within their middle school teaming model.

It would take another book to explain the Option Program but you can find out more about this program on the Recommended Readings/Resource pages at the end of the book.

As for the proposal to implement block scheduling, the pandemic provided a mitigating opportunity to test drive a block schedule because it limited the number of times students moved from class to class on any given day. Being driven by purpose can sometimes result in unintended opportunity.

Chapter Seven Essential Questions:

- What are your stories of challenge, growth and success?
- How do you reflect on your stories and use the lessons learned to continue innovating programs that engage students in meaningful learning?
- How do you celebrate, laugh and remember the tough work that resulted in something special?
- How do you share your stories so that others are inspired?

Spark Doing!

Below is a checklist summarizing the big ideas of this chapter into action steps that you may want to consider.

- Memorialize your stories by documenting your journey.
- Use your stories to relate and express vulnerability when taking on challenges.
- Share your stories at workshops and conferences.
- Take pride in any measure of accomplishment and use it as momentum to
- continue to push the boundaries.

Chapter Eight

Time to Straighten the Curve!

Envision a place where the confines of coverage were obsolete and gave way to depth of understanding, and silos of learning gave way to amalgamation. A place where connections of content and experience less resembled the age of industrialism and more the age of digitization. A place where learning and access to excellence was the right and privilege of all.

We think it important to mention that at the time that this book was being written, we were wrestling with one of the most challenging times we have faced in education, caused by the COVID-19 global pandemic. Then, toward the end of completing this book, the virus mutated causing similar yet different challenges. These unforeseen challenges have become an unlikely and reinforcing impetus to jettison a one size fits all model of learning. We thought it important to mention the pandemic because difficult and sometimes tragic situations can often result in reflection and growth. While a crisis will bring out the worst in us, it will also bring out the best in us—*if we allow it!*

While our vision was clear and the work was being done before the pandemic struck, it forced us to continue reflecting on many of the assumptions that fuel our work. We chose neither to let the pandemic drive us back to industrial model ways of thinking nor allow it to be an excuse for a return to the status quo. Instead, the pandemic further magnified the importance of equity, engagement, agency, purpose and outcomes.

We argue that the techniques and strategies essential to our vision for teaching and learning is an approach that will also help students get through future pandemic type scenarios, without a significant loss to learning. The use of digital learning tools and personal learning devices have become a necessity as we meet the challenges of remote and in-person learning that require distancing.

The pandemic, in many ways, sped up the pace of our journey to develop strategies, techniques, spaces and leadership structures in order to realize our vision of All-Access Learning. The pandemic motivated caring teachers and staff to take risks and learn new techniques more quickly because of the need to keep students engaged during difficult times.

Time to Act!

There has never been a better time to take on the work of transforming our styles of leadership, building capacity and engaging students in relevant and authentic teaching and learning. The research supporting a significant instructional shift away from rote methods is prevalent and pervasive. Instructional technologies are usable and abundant making our work to reimagine instruction more doable than at any other time.

The realization and eagerness on the part of many teachers and staff to change and improve is growing. More and more parents are seeing the mismatch between industrial age pedagogy and the skills and habits of mind that are needed for success after high school.

We wrote this book for those who want to question the traditional practices of an age that is long behind us and do something about it. It is also for those who understand that public education is now in a competitive market and parents are shopping schools. We believe that parents are shopping for the kinds of learning experiences, opportunities and pathways like the ones described in this book.

Our work is not the panacea of improvement and change. While we hope it inspires philosophical discourse, *Straightening The Curve: Designing for Deep Learning and Creating Thriving Learning Communities* is meant to be a real-life example of what can be accomplished and how it can be done. Each school district has its own culture and community values. There is no one way to get it done. However, we believe the principles and practices laid out in this book must be implemented and evolve in some shape or form in order to create a sustainable and flexible model that will drive meaningful and authentic teaching and learning. By way of review, the following summarizes our thoughts, actions and experiences that we have offered in the preceding chapters.

Developing an Actionable Vision

The key mindset here is to resist the notion that a vision is a beautifully worded statement meant for letterhead and public perception. An actionable vision is complex and encompasses the dreams and hopes of those we lead on many levels. All too often we confuse having vision with the crafting of a vision statement. It is a trap to think that the time put into crafting vision statements means the school district has a vision. It is our actions that define the vision.

In our opinion, it is also important to rethink the typical strategic planning process in order to turn a vision into reality. There are many great strategic plans out there and many have produced effective results. However, the typical process has also resulted in many shelved plans with no action. Strategic planning is not a linear process. It is dynamic, organic and can be designed to evolve and adjust. In our view, an actionable vision is one that feels like a continuous moving spiral of interconnected parts.

Short term wins and momentum are key.

Action can occur before, during and as the plan is developing. The actions that define the vision must be systemic and connected to the performance appraisals of leaders and staff. Developing an actionable vision is often done by engaging key stakeholders in large groups and going through a lengthy, watered-down process of consensus. We encourage a different approach. An approach that is intimate and both formal and informal. Smaller groups of stakeholders in welcoming settings with clear purpose and an understanding of the whys will produce amazing insights, wants and needs. There must be an understanding among stakeholders that their involvement is not an opportunity to promote personal agendas and consensus on what will get done is not always possible.

The purpose of stakeholder groups in our process is to help the school leadership prioritize and give insight into what is best for students. We suggest that the discourse and subsequent questions among stakeholders are grounded in these fundamental questions.

- What do we do well?
- How can we do what we do well, better?
- What do we need to change or invent for relevancy?

Leadership must be prepared to act soon once the answers to these questions begin to be answered. We propose acting on the no-brainers before the final version of the actionable vision is completed. This will help achieve short term wins and build trust and momentum. *Remember*—Don't be afraid to fly the plane while it is being built.

The Distributive Leadership Structure

Developing and implementing an actionable vision is futile without a leadership structure that requires leaders to continuously collaborate, constantly communicate, engage at high levels and be innovative, creative, practical and pragmatic. It is our experience that there must be a willingness to resist the urge to work in silos where many find it most comfortable.

This approach to leadership will require respectful yet tough conversations with some individuals who may not share this philosophy and are not interested in adapting. As leaders we owe these folks the opportunity to either demonstrate a willingness to grow or gracefully exit the organization.

The superintendent is responsible for setting the structure and the tone with full support from the board of education. All leaders, formal and informal, must be welcome at the table. It is the vision, purposes, the whys and the work that determine and who sits at the table. The work of school boards, committees, cabinets, advisory councils, administrative teams, teacher-based teams and district leadership teams should be guided by the principles of the Professional Learning Community. It is imperative that leaders trust in the talents of staff, students, parents and community to get the work of improvement and change done. Buy-in and ownership are not only essential but incredibly rewarding.

Team leaders can be permanent or ad hoc depending on the need. The structure of each group should be flexible and be able to adapt and pivot to new challenges as they arise. An investment in professional learning with regards to high functioning teams is absolutely necessary and will boost confidence and productivity. We find that those involved in the meaningful work of leadership at all levels become energized champions of the vision. We have also experienced that for many, it has revitalized and refreshed their careers.

What makes the *Distributive Leadership Structure* work, is the communication thread that is woven throughout all of the groups. Each group must inform the other. For example, if one group is charged with redesigning learning spaces, they should be communicating with those groups charged with reimagining and redesigning instruction so that there is a match between the space and the instructional practices. Another example of this is school board members and the chief financial officer participating in community advisory groups focused on student skill development so that practice can be supported by policy and fiscal stewardship.

Critical to all of the energy, time and hard work of dozens of people is the assurance that well researched risk taking is valued and encouraged. Setting this kind of culture takes time. There will be skepticism and resistance based on past practices and decisions whether real or perceived. Overcoming these hurdles is not rocket science. Key leaders must be present and supportive when things do not go as planned.

The belief that failure is an opportunity must be constantly communicated so that people will try new things and develop those things into effective practices. It is also important that key leaders must take a moment to smell the roses and help others to celebrate accomplishments and what has been learned.

The Responsive Curriculum Framework

As stated throughout this book, the world is changing and will continue to change. These changes require us to prepare students to not only know content but to form habits of mind that allows them to be successful in a world that requires more than industrial age skills.

We believe that quality instruction should be designed and customized to meet the needs of all learners and should be responsive to the creative, innovative, collaborative and problem-solving demands of our constantly changing world. For example, it is no longer sufficient to learn to factor polynomials without understanding its use and being able to apply this knowledge in a collaborative setting to problem solve, innovate or create new knowledge. Student learning and growth is at the heart of our work. What we teach, how we teach it and what students learn starts with the curriculum. Learning basic knowledge and skills is not enough. A curriculum that is not adaptable and responsive to changes in a world that requires deeper learning is not adequate.

An instructional vision for the school district needs to be set before a responsive curriculum can be crafted and implemented. Stakeholders should be involved in setting the instructional course for the district and understand the reasoning for it. Taking the time to involve the board, administrators, teachers, staff, community and students from the outset of the process will build trust, ownership and confidence.

Critical to establishing the culture necessary for crafting a responsive curriculum is assessing the degree to which your district is a learning organization. Whether it is to a greater or lesser degree, the soil needs to be cultivated for the bamboo to grow. Especially important is understanding the capacity of leaders to be an integral part of designing, implementing, evaluating, modifying and committing to a Responsive Curriculum Framework. It is tough work and it is something for which key leaders need to have a deep belief.

Go slow to go fast. This mantra must be spoken many times during the process. Investing in a design and implementation process of authentic collaboration takes time, patience and learning. The quality of a responsive curriculum and its implementation is ultimately determined by the talent and expertise of your teachers and staff. Strategically selected instructional work and action research teams made up of staff, students and when appropriate, community is key. When these teams are guided by knowledgeable and courageous leaders the process will result in a framework that is relevant, rigorous and highly engaging.

Instruction Reimagined

Change is difficult and challenging because it is often deeply personal. In our profession we are all ultimately judged on the quality of what we do in the classroom with students. To a great degree our professional lives are defined by the experiences, failures and successes students have in our classroom. While the process can strain relationships and cause sleepless nights, deep reflection and examination of our practices can be fulfilling and rewarding.

Reimagining instruction is impossible without an actionable, districtwide vision that supports classroom instruction. Classroom instruction should be the heartbeat of any plan to enact improvement and change. Classroom instruction is the center of our professional universe and all organizational aspects must revolve around it and provide it life.

Attempting to change a deeply rooted system of instructional design and practices, that we have spent years implementing over and over again, begs the most common but most unanswered question in education. *Why and for what purpose?*

The journey of reimagining requires the time for teachers, administrators, staff, community, students and parents to reflect and understand the answer to the question. It is especially important that the practitioners responsible for reimagining instruction be given the time for deep thinking and reflection. This cannot be overstated. The opportunity to research, discuss, dream, create and design not only brings intellectual comfort but can be quite inspiring.

It is essential that from the process of reflection comes a set of questions that are continuously used to keep the focus on the practical work of reimagining. These questions are the hard questions that connect the work to the vision, the purpose and the why. These questions should be asked throughout the process and be a way of self-assessing the fidelity of what is intended.

The phenomenon of the status quo and the urge to regress to the mean is tough to overcome. In order to prevent this from happening from the outset pay attention to how work teams and stakeholder committees are spending their time. Leaders need to intervene and refocus the group on the why and the purpose if they are spending more time flexing the status quo muscle for control than designing relevant and responsive instruction. We believe in a representation of stakeholders at the table. However, it may be necessary to have one on one conversations with those who are attempting to gain control and filibuster progress. Strategic formation of teams of varying personalities and skill sets will help to get the work done.

The traditional routines of classroom practice are ingrained in our school cultures. Student voice, choice, relationships, agency, teamwork, opportunity and autonomy often take a back seat to traditional routines of control. In our view these attributes are the foundational principles of reimagined instruction that is customized, relevant and highly engaging.

Support, Support and More Support!

Too often we take for granted the work of supporting those who are in the trenches designing and implementing innovations. Far too often, leaders get bogged down in the day-to-day trials, causing us to lose sight of the necessary work of providing resources, being a resource, encouraging and celebrating small and big accomplishments. We must not assume that those making it happen will continue without thoughtful and purposeful support. It is imperative that the infrastructure of systemic support be firmly in place before, during and after the work reimagining the classroom ecosystem.

We have emphasized over and over again, the challenges of reimagining the classroom ecosystem by designing for deep learning and creating thriving learning communities. It is hard work that takes courage and stamina. However, we want you to know that the journey to get there and the outcomes of the work are also deeply rewarding and gratifying. When the learning culture of the school system shifts to a culture of continuous reflection and action grounded in researched best practices it brings on a sense of professional pride that is exciting to experience.

Seeing and hearing the professional discourse among staff while they create and innovate on a level not often experienced for the purpose of engaging students is awe inspiring. The continuous discussions on how we "get better" brings a vibe that makes working in our profession exhausting, yet fun. Even more inspiring is observing these practices executed in classrooms. For us, it is the level of which students find joy and meaning in their own learning that brings the deepest feelings of professional and personal satisfaction.

Personalized Professional Learning

If we believe that a one size fits all approach to learning for students is no longer relevant then it should no longer be adequate for teachers and staff when it comes to professional learning. It makes little sense to continue an industrial approach to professional learning if our instructional practices are trending toward a customized approach to teaching and learning. The way we learn as professionals must reflect the reality of the classroom culture of personalization and collaboration.

In other words, the entire school culture of learning will shift if we as professionals engage in our own learning in the same manner that we expect students to engage in theirs. Students watch us. They are keenly intuitive if we as mentors, role models and teachers practice what we preach.

There are significant differences between training and professional learning. Training is rote and most often has an endpoint. Professional learning is a continuous process of growth. It must be relevant and meaningful so it does not lead to negative frustration. Professional learning is most effective when teachers and staff can leave a session and use it the next day then bring what they learned to the next session and share expertise.

Each of us in our work lives have a desire to be valued. We also want a say in how we can improve and grow in our jobs. We believe that professional learning programs are best when they are designed by stakeholders in a highly collaborative environment. The concept of "bonded choice" is critical to bringing us together for the purpose of achieving the goals that make up the vision for instruction. This concept of "bonded choice" is about designing relevant and rewarding professional learning toward laser focused goals and a vision that is clearly defined.

The path for achieving the instructional vision is determined through a collaborative process with which teachers, staff, administrators, students and sometimes experts from other professions work together to reimagine instruction within the classroom ecosystem. It's a discussion for another time, but keep in mind that the classroom ecosystem is not limited to what happens within the walls of the classroom and school building.

The bottom line, is that discourse and design are meaningless without action. Being bonded with colleagues in the design process also means a commitment to putting into practice what was learned. Sharing the experiences also helps to improve the professional learning program. Just imagine the level of buy-in, ownership and accountability that would exist after talented and motivated educators designed a personalized professional learning system for your district. We have witnessed first-hand the energy, pride and excitement that the cycle of research, learn, do, assess, adjust and try again generates in the hearts and minds of educators.

Celebrate! Have Fun!

People who work in schools love to socialize. Most educators we know, are high energy and enjoy celebrating. The work of reimagining and transformation is invigorating and exhausting. It pushes staff to their limits. Talented educators often drive themselves toward accomplishment without stopping to smell the roses, laugh and party. However, the work is not only supposed to be something to be proud of, *it is supposed to be fun!* Our leaders find all kinds of ways to celebrate and have a blast! What we have learned from them, is that celebrating should not be a perfunctory event, it should be built in and become a natural part of the culture.

All of our leaders are good at this but there is one that is particularly amazing at finding ways to have a good time at just the right time. Middle school principal Paul Destino is like no one we have ever seen, in developing a fun and happy building culture that demands excellence from students and staff. It's not the obligatory recognition staff meetings that do it. It's the day-to-day smiles, honest conversations, expressions of vulnerabilities and willingness to laugh with one another when something does not go the way it should that has been infused and is now natural to the culture. It's also the food trucks, after work gatherings, staff–student events, crazy dress up days, fun morning announcements and Paul's self-deprecating style that makes those around him want to not only follow his lead, but also take on leadership roles.

Like all of our principals, Paul welcomes dozens of visitors to see our programs and encourages our staff to get on the road to share their expertise across the country. All of our principals build school pride by using student and staff accomplishments as the reason to have some fun together. All of this is seen by staff as affirmation of their work and they have fun doing it. Fun together builds relationships and trust.

Students from all backgrounds are depending on courageous leaders to listen, research, learn and design educational systems and experiences that will provide them with the relationships, knowledge, thinking and people skills that will help them discover and grow their purpose and passion. As important are the thousands of educators and support staff who give all they got for their students. They too depend on leaders to provide opportunities to get better at what they live to do. Even bigger than any of us is the influence we have as an educational community in how we prepare our students to not only solve the challenges of our time but to strive toward taking better care of each other in a shrinking world.

It's Time to Straighten the Curve!

Recommended Readings/Resources

Creating Innovators: The Making of Young People Who Will Change the World, Tony Wagner, Scribner, 2012.

Cultures Built to Last: Systemic PLCs at Work, Richard DuFour, Michael Fulan, Solution Trees Press, 2013.

Dare to Lead; Bave Work. Tough Conversations. Whole Hearts., Brene Brown, Penguin Random House, 2018.

Everyday Courage for School Leaders, Cathay Lasiter, Corwin Press, 2017.

Inventing Better Schools: An Action Plan for Educational Reform, Phillip C. Schlechty, Jossey-Bass, 1997.

Imagine: How Creativity Works, Jonah Lehrer, Houghton Mifflin Harcourt, 2012.

Leading the Inclusive School: Access and Success for All Students, Villa, Richard A. and Thousand, Jaqueline, Association for Supervision and Curriculum Development, 2017.

On Common Ground: The Power of Professional Learning Communities, Richard DuFour, Robert E. Eaker, and Rebecca B. DuFour, National Educational Service, 2005.

Reality Based Leadership, CY Wakeman, Jossey-Bass, 2010.

School Reform from the Inside Out, Richard F. Elmore, Harvard Education Press, 2004.

Team of Rivals, Doris Kearns Goodwin, Simon & Schuster, 2006.

The Brain that Changes Itself, Norman Doidge, MD, Penguin Books, 2007

The Book Whisperer: Awakening the Inner Reader in Every Child, Donalyn Miller and Jeff Anderson, 2009.

The Evolution of Education: Preparing Students for Their Future (Not Our Past), William R. Dagget, International Center for Leadership in Education, 2020.

The Human Side of School Change, Robert Evans, Jossey-Bass, 1996.

The Innovator's Mindset, George Couros, Dave Burgess Consulting, 2015.

The Next Step Forward in Guided Reading: An Assess-Decide-Guide Framework for Supporting Every Reader, Jan Richardson, 2016.

The Power of Moments, Chip Heath and Dan Heath, Simon and Schuster, 2017.

The Option Program—visit www.mayfieldschools.org

About Dr. Keith Kelly

Keith Kelly is a husband, father of five and grandfather of eight. He has served in education for over forty years in high achieving, diverse school districts in the suburbs of Chicago, Cincinnati, and Cleveland. During his four decades plus as an educator, Keith has been a classroom teacher, assistant principal, principal, assistant superintendent, and superintendent. Keith retired as the superintendent of Mayfield City Schools, near Cleveland, Ohio in 2021. He holds two masters' degrees, one in Behavior Disorders and one in Educational Administration from Northeastern Illinois University. He earned his PhD in Educational Leadership and Policy Studies at Loyola University in Chicago. Keith is a fellow at the Center for Educational Leadership at Cleveland State University. Keith is also a graduate of the Harvard Educational Leadership training program and has participated in the Harvard International Think Tank on Education. Keith is currently an educational consultant with American Educational Consultants and K–12 Business Consultants.

About Dr. Patrick Ward

Pat Ward is a husband and a father of three beautiful children. During his twenty-two years as an educator, Pat has been a classroom science teacher, assistant principal, associate principal, high school principal, and director of curriculum. He holds two masters' degrees, one in K-12 Educational Leadership from Ursuline College and one in Curriculum, Instruction and Assessment from Walden University. He earned his PhD in Educational Leadership at Walden University in 2015 with a focus on professional learning communities and school climate. Pat is a fellow at the Center for Educational Leadership at Cleveland State University. He has been recognized by District Administration Magazine for excellent digital leadership and has presented on personalized learning at several national conferences. Also, Pat serves as an adjunct professor at Ursuline college where he teaches courses in curriculum development, instructional coaching and change leadership.